THE FRIENDLY STORE

VICKI INGHAM

THE
History
PRESS

Published by The History Press
Charleston, SC
www.historypress.net

Copyright © 2016 by Vicki L. Ingham
All rights reserved

Cover images: Postcards from the collections of Jean Chamberlain and Diana Schneider.

First published 2016

Manufactured in the United States

ISBN 978.1.46711.995.5

Library of Congress Control Number: 2016933579

CONTENTS

Preface   7
Introduction   9

1. Band of Brothers   11
2. A Branch in Des Moines   16
3. The Largest Store in Iowa   20
4. "As Modern as Tomorrow"   29
5. Supporting the Troops   34
6. Midcentury Expansion   46
7. The Younkers Tea Room   54
8. Furnishing the Iowa Home   65
9. A Full-Service Store   77
10. Iowa's Fashion Capital   87
11. Something Is Always Happening at Younkers   105
12. A Great Place to Work   116
13. Here to Do What Is Right   122
14. The End of Independence   129

Notes   135
Bibliography   147
Index   151
About the Author   155

PREFACE

I moved to Des Moines in 1994 and had lunch in the Tea Room only once, but that was enough to get a sense of what a wonderful place it must have been, full of people and music and things happening on the stage. Much later, I learned about Younkers bringing Halston to town to raise money for the Des Moines Art Center, and I became aware of what a vital institution the store had been in its heyday. When the chance to delve into the company's archival documents came along, it was too tempting an opportunity to pass up.

Younkers: The Friendly Store is primarily the story revealed in those documents, especially in the *Younker Reporter*, the company newsletter published by and for employees. I am very grateful to William Friedman Jr., Elaine Estes and Peter Taggart for sharing their memories and stories with me and to William Peverill for permission to quote from his story about the fashion show in the Younkers Tea Room. Thank you also to the staff of the State Historical Society of Iowa Library, which holds the Younkers archives, and to the Des Moines Public Library research department. In addition, I'm enormously grateful to the following for sharing Younkers memorabilia and images: Connie Boesen, Jean Chamberlain, Diana Schneider, Margaret Rubicam and Jason Eslinger and Heidi Reed of the Iowa Girls Athletic Union. Many thanks to Mary Donahue at Grandview University, Paula Mohr at the State Historic Preservation Office and Katherine Lincoln at Drake University, as well as Mary Gottschalk, Nancy Morton, James H. Windsor III and Carol Bodenstein for their assistance and suggestions. I am very grateful to Dr. Cynthia Ingham for her expert editorial eye, suggestions and sisterly support. Last, but most definitely not least, thank you to Bon-Ton Stores for permission to use the Younkers materials for this book.

PHOTO CREDITS KEY:

CB: Connie Boesen
JC: Jean Chamberlain
MR: Margaret Rubicam
DS: Diana Schneider
IGAU: Iowa Girls Athletic Union
SHSI: Younkers Inc. MS 2003.8 collection, State Historical Society of Iowa, Des Moines
IVHC: The Register Archives/Iowa Visual History Center, Grandview University

INTRODUCTION

Mention Younkers to just about any longtime resident in Des Moines and invariably they'll bring up the Tea Room, with its white tablecloths, chicken salad and cinnamon rolls. Or they'll recall the basement Cremona Room, with the piano player near the entrance and the menu favorite of rarebit burgers with fries and a chocolate malt. The elegant French Room; the elevators with their friendly, uniformed operators; and the music department where you could listen to the latest records all lodged themselves in people's memories and affections.

In the first decades of the twentieth century, almost every town in Iowa had at least one homegrown department store. Des Moines, as the capital city, had dozens. Younkers rose above them all by absorbing its competitors and winning people's loyalty with low prices, high quality, friendly service and an uncompromising commitment to customer satisfaction.

Throughout its history, the company emphasized courteous personal attention, and many customers had "their" sales associate with whom they always did business. One longtime customer recalled that her mother "always bought Helena Rubenstein cosmetics, and she had her own 'lady' at the cosmetic counter." She also had a favorite associate in the women's department who would call her if something she might like came in. Elaine Estes, who interned at the store during college and worked as an associate buyer before graduate school, recalled that whenever her husband needed to buy her a gift, he could go to Flossie (Florence) Miller in the French Room for suggestions—Flossie would know what Elaine liked.[1]

YOUNKERS, DES MOINES — A GREAT STORE SERVING ALL IOWA

Iowa's first block-long department store had a suitably palatial style. *JC.*

Younkers was more than a place to shop and eat, however. You could see fine arts exhibits and attend dances, lectures, cooking demonstrations, book clubs and charm school there. Its corner window featured educational and inspirational displays, and the company was a leader in community philanthropy and civic causes. It was, in a very real sense, a community institution and a model corporate citizen. As the company grew into a regional chain, it carried its principles of customer service and community involvement into towns across the Midwest.

In many ways, Younkers reflected the traditional values of its midwestern context. At the same time, it aimed to be at the forefront of whatever was new and fashionable. Its buyers and executives studied what retail leaders in the big cities did, and when Younkers introduced new practices or merchandising ideas to Iowa, it went with the best—top-name suppliers and designers and top-quality materials, both for merchandise and for store improvements.

No matter how successful the company became, management and employees never forgot its roots. Every year, the autumn Anniversary Sale celebrated the store's history and pointed with pride to its special place in the lives of Iowans. For most of its history, Younkers really was the store for all Iowa. It prospered along with the state and was proud to be a part of its growth.

Chapter I

BAND OF BROTHERS

Like many department stores in the United States, Younkers started out as a dry goods store established by Jewish immigrants. In the mid-1800s, six Younker brothers, born in Lipno, Poland, made their way to the Midwest in search of opportunity. The two eldest, Benjamin and Lipman, arrived first and settled in Louisiana, Missouri, in 1851 or 1852 (sources disagree). Samuel (age seventeen) and Marcus (age fifteen) arrived in New York City in 1854. Younger brothers Manassa and Joseph and two half-brothers, Herman and Aaron, followed later.

They apparently arrived in America with little more than their wits and some knowledge of trade. Many years later, Marcus recalled, "I had a stock of stationery amounting to $2.50 to start my career in this country with." As he was climbing onto a stage to Union Square, where he would sell the stationery either to passersby or door to door in office buildings, he dropped the stationery in the muddy gutter. "Kind-hearted bystanders had remorse upon me and helped me out with the sum of one dollar and that practically was my start in the United States," he wrote.[2] After a few unsuccessful years in the city, Samuel and Marcus traveled to Keokuk, Iowa, where Lipman had moved in 1855. The three brothers opened a dry goods store, Younker & Bros., in 1856, leasing the first floor of 82 Main Street.[3]

Nestled between the Des Moines and Mississippi Rivers and lying just south of impassable rapids on the Mississippi, Keokuk prospered as a terminal port for riverboats carrying goods and freight up from St. Louis. The Des Moines River, though unpredictable, remained an important way to move

Lipman, Samuel and Marcus Younker, the company's founders. *SHSI.*

Keokuk, Iowa, gateway to the Midwest in the mid-1800s.

goods into the interior, and as the gateway to this region, Keokuk promised opportunities for growing numbers of entrepreneurs and merchants. Settlers moving west in large convoys of covered wagons passed through Keokuk and stopped for supplies. By 1856, the town was prosperous enough to install gas streetlights, and the *Daily Gate City* newspaper noted that citizens were busy organizing a Republican party, attending the occasional theatrical production and listening to Lyceum lectures.[4]

Keokuk also had the largest Jewish population in the young state. Most were merchants, either of dry goods or clothing; one was a physician. In 1855, they established a mutual aid society to help the sick and bury the dead. By 1863, there were enough faithful to form a congregation, which met above the Younker & Bros. store. In 1876, the first synagogue in Iowa was built in Keokuk with the help of the Younker brothers.[5]

The Younker & Bros. store, Marcus recalled, "carried a little bit of everything" and served settlers living as far west as Eddyville and Ottumwa. "They were hard days, but we had good patronage, and our greatest trouble was in establishing credit with eastern wholesale houses," he wrote. Sometimes they had to take whatever the buyer sent them. "Once our buyer cleared out the remnant of a stock of bowie knives and shipped them west to us…When the knives came, we unpacked them and found ten or twelve dozen." Faced with what seemed an absurdly large number of knives, they debated whether to send them back to New York but decided instead to display a few in the window. "One day the driver of a prairie schooner came to our store, noticed the knives in the windows, and asked their price. We told him $2.00 apiece. 'Have you got many?' he asked. We told him we had a good stock…A few minutes later, fifty or sixty men came over from the emigrant train and they bought every knife in the store."[6]

In addition to selling from the store, the brothers used the shop as a base for going out into the countryside of Lee and Des Moines Counties as itinerant peddlers. According to company history, they stayed with farmers in the Des Moines River Valley and paid for their bed and board with merchandise. The packs were as large as steamer trunks, loaded with bolts of cloth, sewing notions and sundries, and each man carried one on his back.[7]

When the Civil War began in 1861, most of the Iowa regiments set off from Keokuk. In addition to a military camp, the town hosted six war hospitals, and eventually a national cemetery was established. Manassa's son Isaac remembered his father saying that the store kept busy looking after the needs of the soldiers who passed through.[8]

Re-creation of Younkers' first newspaper ad in Keokuk, 1864.

Sometime during the first year of the war, Lipman, by now twenty-seven years old, returned to New York City to marry Gertrude Cohen, the daughter of a Polish rabbi. Two years later, in 1863, Samuel married Gertrude's sister, Ernestina (Tina), and brought her back to Keokuk. Marcus married his cousin Anna Berkson in New Orleans in 1868.[9]

In 1864, Younker & Bros. took out its first newspaper ad in the *Daily Gate City*. The notice alerted the public to its selection of dry goods "for sale at the very lowest market prices," including black and colored silks, "Merinos and Alpacas, Shawls and Cloaks, Blankets and Quilts, Yarns and Hosieries, Carpets and Oil Cloths, Which will be sold at prices to correspond with the late decline in gold." The ad also stated that "special notice is given that our store will be closed on every Saturday," allowing the brothers to keep the Sabbath.

On August 29, 1866, the first passenger train from Keokuk to Des Moines made its maiden run, and Samuel was among the forty residents of Keokuk making the seven-and-a-half-hour trip to the capital city. When the train pulled into the station at East Fifth and Market, the travelers were treated like celebrities, with speeches, a parade and a brass band. The passengers spent the night either at the Savery Hotel (then at Fourth and Walnut) or the Demoine House.[10] Presumably, Samuel went to investigate expansion opportunities but must have returned unimpressed. The family didn't stake a claim in the retail business there until 1874.

Although Lipman had arrived in Keokuk first, it was Samuel who took the lead in running the store. This may have created some tension between the equally entrepreneurial brothers. In addition to participating in the dry goods store, Lipman opened his own shop in 1868, L.M. Younker & Company, selling gentlemen's clothes and furnishings. His youngest brother, Joseph, had arrived in Keokuk two years earlier to begin working at the main store, and then he joined Lipman as a clerk. In March 1870,

Lipman officially dissolved the partnership with Samuel and Marcus and focused on his clothing store. Sometime before 1879, Lipman moved his store to Des Moines, setting up shop at 319 Walnut Street, and moved his family to New York.[11]

During the early 1870s, Younkers continued to promote fabrics, dress goods, table linens "and everything else pertaining to a First Class Dry Goods Store," but now stylishness was mentioned along with rock-bottom prices. Samuel went to New York himself to buy merchandise, and for the 1874 Christmas sale, he brought back "all classes of dry goods suitable for Holiday Presents. We are receiving new goods every day, bought purposely for this special sale and bought for cash at such prices that we are enabled to offer everybody unprecedented bargains." Furs; dress goods such as shawls, blankets and felt skirts; and "Domestic and Housekeeping Goods of every kind at Immense Bargains," along with gloves, underwear, notions and "Fancy Goods of every kind in endless variety," were all on offer at "prices to astonish."[12]

In May 1879, just a week after a family reunion, Samuel became ill with severe diarrhea. He suffered for about ten days before dying of "congestion of the bowels and stomach." Marcus was in New York about to embark on a trip to Europe when he received the news and returned immediately to Keokuk for the funeral. All of the brothers except Lipman attended the services, held at the synagogue that Samuel had helped build three years before. Samuel's obituary in the *Daily Gate City* on May 22 noted that he had been vice-president of B'nai Israel, a member of the congregation's school board and "an enthusiastic B'nai B'rith over which body, in this city, he was president…[A]n influential member of the Hebrew Congregation, [he] enjoyed the respect and confidence not only of his Hebrew fellow citizens, but of all who knew him, and was regarded as a man without an enemy."[13]

Tina and Marcus kept the store operating for about six years after Samuel died. Then they closed shop and moved to Des Moines to join Marcus's half-brother Herman. Manassa Younker and his children continued operating the M. Younker store in Keokuk until 1924. Joseph had opened a store in Bonaparte called Younker & Sonshine in about 1877 but moved his family to east Des Moines in 1884 and opened a dry goods store there in the center of the Jewish community.[14] Thus, the Younker name stood for honest merchandise at low prices in several Iowa towns, but it would be Herman's store that would become a community institution in the state and beyond.

Chapter 2

A BRANCH IN DES MOINES

When Samuel Younker visited Des Moines in 1866, he found twenty-two dry goods stores already in operation. Since Des Moines had about the same population as Keokuk at that time, Samuel apparently thought the town was too small, with too much competition, to risk opening a store there. Eight years later, however, the population in Des Moines was on its way to doubling, and the number of dry goods stores had dropped to seventeen.[15]

Samuel's sixteen-year-old half-brother, Herman, had arrived in Keokuk from Poland in 1870. After four years in training with his older half-brothers, he was ready to go to Des Moines to open a branch store. Most of his competitors were clustered on Walnut Street, so Herman rented a one-story room twenty-two feet wide and sixty feet deep near the corner of Sixth and Walnut. His first ad, appearing in the October 3, 1874 *Iowa State Register*, consisted of three lines of text sandwiched between reports on a thief's arraignment and September arrests: "We have come to live here, and mean to do what is right. If you want honest goods at bottom prices, call at Younker Brothers. McCain's Block, Cor. 6th and Walnut."

According to family history, Herman's nephew, Aaron, age ten, came with him to Des Moines, although the city directory doesn't list Aaron until 1879.[16] In 1876, Herman's cousin Barney joined him as a clerk, and in 1877, the Younkers moved the store a block east to 423 Walnut while they enlarged and remodeled the original building to take in both 515 and 517 Walnut. They returned to that location in 1881 and remained there for eighteen years. Ads placed in the *Des Moines Register* during this period emphasized the store's variety of stock and low prices with those alluring words, "Finest, Largest and Cheapest."[17]

Meanwhile, by 1879, Lipman had opened the short-lived L.M. Younker & Company at 319 Walnut, selling men's clothing and related goods.[18] Because he was living in New York, he left the running of the store to thirty-one-year-old Morris Wilchinski and a nephew, Albert Younker. When he was a toddler, Wilchinski, along with his older sister, Anja, had accompanied Lipman and Benjamin to America. Anja married Benjamin, and Morris would later marry Agnes Berkson, a cousin of the Younker brothers. Their son Norman would become one of the

Herman Younker, founder of the Des Moines branch. *SHSI.*

most beloved presidents in the history of Younkers.[19]

In 1880, Herman Younker made news by hiring the first woman clerk in Des Moines. Mrs. Mary McCann, a thirty-year-old widow, had no work experience outside the home and was nervous about the job. Years later, she said that she stayed at the rear of the store at first, "feeling entirely strange and out of place in this business world dominated by men." Soon, however, female customers began "seeking her out, because they liked the idea of being waited on by a woman. Her success was so decided that a good deal of jealousy was felt among the men." They were less than helpful, but Mary remembered that Mr. Younker became "her friend and tutor and daily gave her valuable lessons in selling, especially introducing new merchandise."[20]

In some cities in the late nineteenth century, female clerks were frowned upon as being of a lower class or of dubious character, but that wasn't the case in Des Moines. After about a year, Mary McCann was joined by other women, including Margaret Cummins, the sister of Albert B. Cummins, future state senator, governor and U.S. senator. Not long after, applicants included former teachers and a former assistant in a dentist's office.[21]

In the early 1880s, store personnel worked long hours, from 7:00 a.m. to 11:00 p.m. In the 1890s, opening was pushed back to 7:45 a.m., but overtime pay was still unheard of. As one longtime employee recalled, workers were "checked in at the door in the morning and fined one cent for every minute we were late."[22] Wages were $2.50 per week for cash girls, stock girls and millinery apprentices. Men apparently earned $3.00 to $3.50 per week.[23] On the other hand, the staff was small enough that "everyone in the store knew each other and on hot summer days a pitcher of lemonade was passed around." Sometimes on winter evenings, Margaret Cummins prepared an oyster supper for the staff. "After the oysters, followed dancing for which Mr. Aaron Younker played the violin and 'called off.'" On Christmas Eve, the small group of employees would file into Herman Younker's office to receive their Christmas gifts. Mrs. McCann remembered that her first gift was a copy of *The Count of Monte Cristo*, and the second year she received a silk umbrella.[24]

In the 1880s and 1890s, many customers arrived at the store in horse-drawn buggies. Sam Hicks, the "carriage man," would greet each carriage, tie up the horses and help the ladies out of their buggies, carefully lifting the trains of their skirts over the wheels and keeping them out of the dust as he escorted them to the door. Dressed in a long blue coat and wearing a flower in his lapel, "he was politeness personified" and "was for years an essential part of the store's service."

Although customers might arrive in a buggy, they did not carry their purchases home with them. Rather, the store delivered the packages to the customer's address. Before 1900, Younkers had a single delivery wagon to serve customers west of the river. To handle deliveries on the east side, the store relied on its cash boys—teenagers who worked all day taking money to the cashier and then swept out the store at closing and delivered packages on their way home. One veteran employee remembered starting to work for the store as a cash boy at age twelve, earning eight dollars per month. According to another former cash boy, "In those days, as now [1926], it was a real honor to work for Younkers. They were very strict and required good references."

In 1893, Herman Younker moved to New York to take over the company's office there but continued as president. Over the course of his career, he came to be regarded as a pioneer in retailing, "one of the best judges of merchandise and merchandise values in the country," according to the *Dry Goods Economist*. "It was his idea that a store ought to reflect all that is best in its personnel and that a store was in a sense a public institution as much as it was a private enterprise."[25]

Marcus retired from the business in 1895, leaving Samuel's sons—Aaron, Falk J. and Isaac—to run the company under Herman. Aaron took over as general manager, Falk J. worked as a manager and Isaac as a department manager. A longtime employee later recalled "how the brothers, Mr. Aaron, Mr. Falk, and Mr. Isaac would come to work in a surrey with the fringe on top," driven by a black coachman. Falk was remembered by another veteran Younkerite as a practical joker who "created a sensation among employees and customers by putting a sack of oatmeal in the water cooler on the first floor."[26]

It was still very much a family business. Ella Costello, who started as a clerk in notions in 1893, remembered "when Mr. Falk Younker used to meet the customers at the door and shake hands with them."[27] A nephew, Albert, clerked in the store, and Joseph, the youngest full brother of the founders, had closed his eastside shop in 1890 and joined the family store as a salesman. Norman Wilchinski started as a messenger boy at age fifteen; his sister, Lenore, worked as a bookkeeper.[28]

In the 1890s, Des Moines had a population of more than fifty thousand. Drake University, founded in 1881, was followed by Highland Park College, Grandview College and the S.S. Still College of Osteopathy in the last decade of the century. The city had opera houses, a thriving business district, dozens of handsome houses of worship and elegant new neighborhoods going up. Des Moines was growing, and Younkers prospered right along with it.

Chapter 3

THE LARGEST STORE IN IOWA

At the end of the nineteenth century, Younkers faced competition from three other department stores, as well as from fourteen dry goods stores and assorted men's and women's specialty clothing shops. Younkers, Frankel's and Harris-Emery Company all lined Walnut Street. Blotcky Brothers served the east side of town. The three Walnut Street stores vied with one another for preeminence, and their fates became inextricably intertwined.

Frankel's, like Younkers, started in a small town. Isaiah Frankel, a Jewish immigrant from Bavaria, arrived in the United States in 1855 and settled in Oskaloosa, where he opened a bank and a clothing store. In 1894, his sons Nathan and Manassa moved to Des Moines and opened a branch of the clothing store at 413 Walnut. Their brother, Anselm, and brother-in-law Meyer Rosenfield joined them, and in 1899, the family took the leap into the department store business. They invested in a new five-story building on the northeast corner of Sixth and Walnut.[29]

When the store burned to the ground two years later, Rosenfield and the Frankel brothers found themselves nearly broke. With generous loans from a friendly banker and a cousin, the Frankels and Rosenfield bought a controlling interest in the Harris-Emery department store.[30]

Harris-Emery had burst on the scene in 1892, boasting that it was "the largest retail house in the state, retailers of everything direct from the manufacturer to the consumer."[31] Its five-story building anchored the southeast corner of Seventh and Walnut and offered an extensive inventory of merchandise, from china, silverware and household goods in the basement to dress goods, notions, men's and boys' clothing, millinery, shoes, candies and soda water on the first through third floors. On the fourth floor were dressmakers, restrooms and dressing rooms for the ladies, as well as a restaurant. The fifth floor was leased to a furniture company. The store also offered its customers the convenience of a first-floor telegraph and telephone office and post office.

One of the Harrises behind Harris-Emery, Hardy C. Harris, had been in the dry goods business in Des Moines since 1866, when he clerked at George R. Osgood's dry goods store. The other Harris was his cousin Henry, with whom he had opened H.C. Harris & Company, a dry goods store at 618 West Locust in about 1886. Henry then partnered with John Emery to open the new department store, issuing a direct challenge to Younkers, which still lacked many of the amenities and services that Harris-Emery offered.[32]

As if in answer to the challenge, Younkers decided to build a brand-new store just west of Harris-Emery and leased the quarter block on the northwest corner of Seventh and Walnut. Years later, company legend asserted that the business community buzzed with comment over the risky move west of the retail district. In fact, though, it was just diagonally across the street from the Harris-Emery Department House.

The Younkers quarter-block was already built up with two-story commercial structures, a frame house and the original St. Paul's Episcopal Church. The firm hired Weitz Brothers to demolish the existing buildings and build the new store, working with the local architectural firm Liebbe, Nourse & Rasmussen. The *Daily Capital* predicted that the project would prove to the nation that "Des Moines architects and contractors are second to none in completing the erection of such a building. In every respect it is to be finished with an elaborateness of detail for comfort and convenience that is to be found in its counterparts in New York or Chicago. Twenty-three toilet rooms will be scattered about the building and there will be waiting rooms for the rest and comfort of the patrons."[33]

Demolition began on April 8, 1899, and construction proceeded rapidly until October 3, when the Harris-Emery department store caught fire. The intense heat damaged Younkers' cornice and nearly all of its plate glass windows, worth some $4,000. Fortunately, the company had just taken out insurance, so the loss was covered.[34]

Younkers' new store finally opened to the public on November 9, 1899, after a week of moving stock from the old location. Three daily

Completed in 1899, Younkers anchored the northwest corner of Walnut and Seventh Streets. Note the rooftop sign: "Younkers Dry Goods and Carpets." *JC.*

papers published detailed reports of the store's "mammoth, and elegant new home." The *Des Moines Daily News* gushed that "the five floors and basement are fitted up in royal fashion. Nothing like it can be found in the west and no finer establishment graces New York, Chicago or any other city." The *Daily Iowa Capital* praised the novelty and style of the Italian Renaissance exterior, with brick and terra-cotta walls on a skeleton of steel columns and beams. Ornamental iron window mullions were lauded as modern, but the large plate glass windows inspired the most admiration, described as "the finest plate glass," "elegant" and "wonderful." Prism glass transoms on the east façade "make the large rooms as light as day." The basement extended out under the surrounding sidewalks, requiring the company to embed glass skylights into the sidewalks to provide natural light to the subterranean spaces.[35]

Inside, first-floor ceilings soared twenty feet high, supported by seven rows of seven two-foot-square columns. Ceilings were lower on the upper floors, from fifteen feet on the second and third floors to just under fifteen feet on the fifth, but still created a lofty effect. With a total floor space of ninety thousand square feet, the store was described as "the largest and most complete in the city and in fact west of Chicago."[36]

A balcony at the north end framed the two electric elevators and was furnished with comfortable seating and writing desks. Electric and gas lighting, steam heat and ventilation brought modern comfort to the interiors, and pneumatic tubes, the latest in technological wizardry, whisked cash to the cashier's desk, replacing the cash boys and girls. New departments included house furnishings (china, glassware, lamps and so on), jewelry, ladies' and children's shoes, furniture and boys' and children's clothing. The larger store would require three hundred employees and a fleet of new delivery trucks.

The *Des Moines Leader* stated that the "magnificent establishment" would "not be a department house, but, strictly speaking, a dry goods house carrying only such lines as are ordinarily carried in the larger dry goods houses throughout the country…In fact, it is to be a store for ladies and is intended to be able to supply the category of female wants."[37] The variety of merchandise, conveniences and services, however, greatly exceeded the textiles and sundries typical of dry goods stores and certainly put Younkers in the same category as the great department stores back east and in Chicago.

For ten years, the store towered majestically over the two- and three-story buildings filling the rest of the block. In 1909, Younkers hired the architectural firm of Proudfoot, Bird & Rawson to add two more bays on the north side and a sixth floor to the entire building.[38]

Retail development continued to move west, and in 1908, F.M. Hubbell, who owned the quarter block west of Younkers, decided to replace the assorted buildings on the property with a new structure designed for two occupants. Named the Wilkins Building for its primary occupant, the Wilkins Department Store, it was designed by Chicago architect Edwin Arthur Rush and was the first reinforced-concrete (and thus fireproof) commercial building in Des Moines. (In fact, it survived the devastating fire in 2014.)[39]

The Wilkins store had been founded as the Fair Store in east Des Moines in 1881 by Captain Wilkins. The firm moved over to the west side of the river in 1900 and operated as Wilkins Brothers Company at 614–18 Walnut for eight years. In the new, enlarged space at the corner of Eighth and Walnut, the store offered custom draperies and curtains, hand-painted china, rugs, readymade draperies and wallpaper, as well as millinery, coats and suits, men's furnishings, hair goods, women's and children's shoes, domestics and canned goods. Chapman Brothers Furniture Store occupied the two bays closest to Younkers.[40]

As the Wilkins store was going up west of Younkers, the Grand Department Store moved into the 1876 Iowa Exhibition Building, also in

Walnut Street looking east, 1910. Wilkins department store and Chapmans furniture share the Younkers block. The Grand Department Store would be bought out by Younkers in 1912. *CB.*

the 800 block of Walnut. The Grand didn't last long, however. The owners decided to concentrate on their wholesale business in St. Paul and sold their inventory to Younkers in 1912.[41]

After nearly fifteen years in business at the Eighth and Walnut site, the Wilkins store began to falter, and Wilkins Brothers decided not to renew the lease when it expired in 1923. Hubbell approached Younkers about leasing the entire building, and the company agreed. Norman Wilchinski, who had assumed the presidency of Younker Brothers in 1919, noted that the store was squeezed for space and had contemplated moving to a new location. Now Younkers not only would stay put but also would have two blocks of windows, "the largest store frontage in the state of Iowa, and one of the largest in the middle west," said Wilchinski.[42] Ultimately, E.J. Wilkins, president of Wilkins Brothers, decided to sell the store's stock to Younkers rather than open a new store elsewhere, and so another competitor was removed from the scene.

The Great New Store

For Younkers, taking over the Wilkins Building marked a milestone—now the store could greatly expand its furniture, home furnishings and appliance departments, as well as those for men and boys, misses and girls and draperies and rugs. Connecting the two buildings took some architectural juggling. A floor was added to the Wilkins Building, and a four-story bridge over the alley between the two stores connected selling spaces. A marble and bronze storefront unified the façades.[43]

In July 1924, Younkers held a series of moving sales to dispose of the Wilkins stock. In August and September, it promoted its expansion with a series of ads urging customers to "[w]atch this store" and announcing special Expansion Sales as each floor, reorganized and redecorated, reopened to shoppers.

In 1926, Younkers bought out the inventory of another competitor, the Emporium Store, which had been in business on Walnut Street for thirteen years. This acquisition was eclipsed by an even bigger merger with one of its last remaining rivals, Harris-Emery.

Younkers in 1924, joined to the Wilkins Building with a four-floor connector over the alley. *JC.*

Joseph Rosenfield, Meyer's son, recalled that Harris-Emery and Younkers were "fierce competitors. They zealously guarded all their trade secrets from each other, although I suspect that each store exactly knew what the other store was doing all of the time. They hired the other store's clerks, buyers and even executives…All the while, however, the top executives of both businesses were good friends and mingled socially in a very friendly and cordial manner."[44]

In 1923, all department stores in Des Moines had done well in terms of sales volume and net profits, but just three years later, net profits were half what they had been. Heavily dependent on agriculture, the state's economy prospered or suffered according to the level of agricultural prices, and in 1926, prices were low and banks were failing. Late that year, Manassa Frankel of Harris-Emery approached Norman Wilchinski and suggested a merger with Younkers. Although Harris-Emery's assets were smaller than those of Younkers, its management "insisted on receiving 50 percent of the voting stock in the merged corporation," Joseph Rosenfield wrote later. The attorney handling the merger devised a novel solution, placing all of the voting power in "a special issue of 7 percent non-callable preferred stock."[45] Each party to the merger received $500,000 worth of these shares. Younker stockholders received a majority of the non-voting preferred stock and common stock. This arrangement endured until 1948, when Younker Brothers went public and all stock became voting.

After the merger was finalized in January 1927, Meyer Rosenfield joined the Younkers board as vice-president. (He died in 1929 and was succeeded on the board by his son, Joseph.)[46] Rosenfield's brother-in-law, Henry Frankel, joined the Younkers board as secretary and treasurer, and Norman Wilchinski continued as president of the merged company.

A CHANGE IN OWNERSHIP

The final acquisition of the era came in 1928, when J. Mandelbaum & Sons moved its inventory over to Younkers and closed its store. By this time, however, it was the Mandelbaums who owned Younkers, having acquired majority control of the stock in 1923.

Herman and Aaron Younker had incorporated Younker Brothers in 1904 to raise cash for expansion and were the majority stockholders until 1914. After 1908, when Aaron moved to Chicago to start his own business, uncle and nephew continued as president and vice-president of the board of directors but weren't involved in the day-to-day running of the store. Aaron's brothers, Isaac and Falk J., sold their stock and left the company in 1910 and 1912, respectively. Herman's son, Ira M., acquired a significant block of voting shares, as did Norman Wilchinski and another director, Martin H. Burns (a Younker buyer from 1899 to 1917 and vice-president of Harris-Emery from 1917 to 1924).[47]

In 1915, Herman, Aaron and Ira M. still held large blocks of shares and served on the board, but Norman Wilchinski owned the largest number of voting shares. Other Younker family members had continued to work at the store: Samuel's son Isaac was in charge of ready-to-wear until 1910; Joseph Younker worked as a salesman and buyer until his death at age seventy-one in 1918; and his son Albert worked as a clerk, buyer and divisional merchandise manager until about 1926, when he left to go into business for himself. When Herman died in 1920 and Aaron disposed of his shares in 1921, it seems likely that Wilchinski realized the company might be up for grabs and alerted his in-laws, the Mandelbaums, to the opportunity.

Julius Mandelbaum had immigrated to the United States at age fifteen and was about thirty-one years old when he arrived in Des Moines during the Civil War. He and N.L. Goldstone opened a dry goods and clothing store on Court Avenue in 1864. Later, he partnered with G. Jacobs and then Isaac

Walnut Street, 1920s. *JC.*

27

Baum. By 1899, he was operating J. Mandelbaum & Sons, still listed as a dry goods store, at 503–5 Walnut and had been joined in the business by his sons, Morris and Sidney.[48]

When the Mandelbaum sons married Norman Wilchinski's sisters, Lenore and Estelle, family ties linked the two competing stores. Because the Wilchinskis were related to the Younkers through their mother (a cousin of the Younkers), company leadership still tied back to the founders. But when Wilchinski and the Mandelbaums acquired a controlling interest in the corporation in 1923, ownership passed out of the founding family. Julius died that July, and Sidney joined Younkers as vice-president and general manager. Morris continued to run J. Mandelbaum & Sons Inc. until 1928.

Acquisitions like this were not unusual, and as with other such takeovers, the new owners stayed in the background, keeping the name and preserving the history of the acquired store. Every autumn, anniversary celebrations reminded employees and the public of the Younker brothers' story, burnishing the living legacy of those pioneering Polish immigrants. The first generation had established the policy of high quality, low prices and good service and had set the pace for growth. The new owners—Norman Wilchinski, the Mandelbaums, the Frankels and the Rosenfields—turned Younkers into a community institution and built it into the store for all of Iowa and beyond.

Chapter 4

"AS MODERN AS TOMORROW"

While Younkers embraced the idea of being progressive and modern, its management usually preferred to study what stores did elsewhere and see what worked before risking change. Within the state, however, the store aimed to stay ahead of its competition with new ideas and practices. A slogan adopted for the Diamond Jubilee in 1931 captured the store's forward-looking ambitions: "Seventy-Five Years Old and as Modern as Tomorrow."[49]

Up-to-date amenities in the 1899 building—such as restrooms, lounges and tearooms for customers' comfort and convenience—won praise, but installing air conditioning in 1936 put the store in a whole new category of modernity. Like department stores everywhere, Younkers' management had struggled with enticing customers to shop during the stifling heat of summer. Until 1902, the only practical options were open windows and electric fans.

In 1902, however, the New York Stock Exchange and an office building in Kansas City installed air conditioning systems, and the public enjoyed its first experience of the new technology at the St. Louis World's Fair. By 1917, movie theaters were luring wilting patrons with the promise of brisk, refreshing temperatures inside. The first department store to install air conditioning was J.L. Hudson in Detroit in 1924. Filene's in Boston followed soon after, but both stores cooled only the basement and main floor.[50]

Younkers was one of the first to air-condition the entire store, including workrooms, stockrooms and the basement shipping room across the alley. To design the system, the company hired Charles S. Leopold, the nationally

In 1935, a continuous eleven-foot-wide metal canopy was installed above the display windows. *CB.*

recognized consultant who was also working on air conditioning for the Capitol in Washington, D.C., and had designed the systems for Gimbell's, Saks, Sears and Maison Blanche.[51]

Company president Henry Frankel enumerated the benefits of air conditioning to employees, inadvertently highlighting just how unpleasant the work environment must have been—hot and steamy, with soot drifting in through open windows to dirty the merchandise and coat every surface with dust and grit. "Improved working conditions for all employees, in the service departments as well as the selling floors, having them work in complete comfort the year round, means greater efficiency," he wrote. "Sealed windows and washed air the year round means a cleaner store.… The customer can stay in the store all day in perfect comfort with a better relationship between customer and employee."[52]

Investing in this top-of-the-line system put Younkers ahead of its competitors in Iowa and made it one of the more progressive stores nationwide. Even nine years later, according to the *New York Times*, just one in ten department stores had undertaken the expense of installing air conditioning.[53]

ELECTRIC STAIRS

Three years after installing the cooling system, Younkers took its next big step in modernization: escalators. Getting customers to go beyond the first floor had been a problem for department stores everywhere. At Younkers, customers had initially been reluctant to use the hydraulic elevators installed in the 1880s. The new store built in 1899 hoped to encourage shoppers upstairs with elegant electric elevators staffed by uniformed operators. But even with that inducement, a 1919 industry report showed that only slightly more than one-quarter of those entering a multilevel store went beyond the first floor.[54]

Moving stairs, or escalators, promised to change that. Bloomingdale's installed an early escalator invented by Jesse Reno in 1898, but other stores were slow to follow its lead, due to the expense and the still-developing technology.[55] Through the mid-1920s and into the 1930s, design and technology continued to improve. Nevertheless, even in 1939, when Younkers unveiled its own moving stairs, escalators were still such a novelty that a local radio station broadcast the opening ceremony live, and thousands lined up to take a ride. The store chose the Westinghouse brand, similar to the ones at Marshall Field's in Chicago. "They are the only ones of their kind in Iowa, and one of the few in the Midwest," noted the *Younker Reporter*.[56]

It is hard to imagine now the wonder and excitement the electric stairs provoked. The ribbon-cutting ceremony on the evening of October 20 opened with a Younkers customer describing for listeners "what is perhaps the most dramatic event in the shopping history of Iowa. In the limelight of course, is this dazzling escalator or moving stairway.… Its beauty beggars

Crowds wait for a chance to ride the first escalator in Iowa on October 10, 1939. *SHSI.*

description! Enclosed in glistening nickel-bronze and marble base, it rises majestically to the second floor. From there a set of two moving stairways lead to the third floor…one for upgoing passengers…the other down."[57] (Riding down from the second to the main floor required making your way to the west building.)

Employees had enjoyed a sneak preview the morning before, with 20-Year Club members taking the first ride. Barney Barnard and his orchestra accompanied community singing that must have included the ditty published later in the *Younker Reporter*, "New Escalator Song," to be sung to the tune of "Take Me Out to the Ball Game":

> *Let's go up on the stairway*
> *Let's go up with the crowd*
> *No more rushing to catch a car*
> *All you do is just stand where you are—and you*
> *Ride right up to the third floor*

And see the brand new display
And it's one, two, three steps and you're down
On the new stair way.[58]

As with air conditioning, so with Iowa's first moving stairway: the innovations conferred prestige and good publicity. "These changes are going to make shopping very much more convenient for our customers," said Frankel, "and undoubtedly will result in increased sales volume. We have always found that as we give added service and facilities to the public, the customer in turn pays us back with increased purchases."[59]

CHARGE IT, PLEASE

In September 1940, Younkers took its customers one step closer to the future with the Charga-Plate system, precursor to store credit cards. While the plates eliminated the need to hand-write a customer's name and address on the receipt, the equipment sometimes presented its own problems—a bent plate or worn-out ink roller produced an illegible image, for example—and customers apparently needed some persuasion to adopt them as a matter of course. In 1956, training director Mabel Kutch was still offering associates tips on how to subtly encourage customers to use their Charga-Plates.[60]

With the introduction of cycle billing, Younkers' systems were up to date and ready to take the store into the future. Then the war came.

Chapter 5

SUPPORTING THE TROOPS

Younkers had established itself as a community institution by 1899, but during World War II, it soared to new heights of civic leadership. Henry Frankel's message to employees on December 9, 1941, one day after Congress declared war on Japan, laid out the store's mission for the duration: "Younkers has a duty to perform in war time greater than it ever had in peace time…Now is the time to hold the morale of the Younker family at the highest level…This is the time for greater friendliness and cooperation—for added courage, confidence and cheerfulness." Frankel acknowledged that federal taxes would be high for both businesses and individuals for years to come. "The cost of the job will be immense. No matter what the price, we're committed to pay it—and we will, not with grumbling and complaint, but with the sincere feeling that we're all partners in America, ready and happy to do our part."[61]

FINANCING THE WAR

His patriotism-over-profits message echoed that of retailers across the country, and like other retailers, Younkers soon had the chance to prove that it was sincere. The U.S. Treasury Department enlisted businesses to help finance the war by selling bonds and stamps. Series E bonds, aimed at individual investors, sold for as little as $18.75 and would pay $25.00 at maturity forty years later. Series F and G bonds, which were more expensive and matured in twelve years, were also issued. War stamps cost $0.10 each and allowed people who couldn't afford a bond to collect the stamps in a special album until they had enough to trade for a bond.[62]

An enormous nationwide marketing effort went into promoting the bonds and stamps. Movie stars, sports figures and artists lent their celebrity to the campaigns, and advertising agencies donated their services. By the end of the war, more than 85 million Americans had purchased bonds amounting to $185.7 billion.[63]

As an employer, Younkers was charged by the U.S. Treasury Department to encourage all its employees to buy war bonds through payroll deduction. By February 1942, the store employees' participation in the Retailers for Victory campaign was just a little over one-third of its workforce, so management appointed the 20-Year Club to take on the job of achieving 100 percent involvement. "Every employee should consider it his first duty to take part in the all-out effort to win the war," admonished the *Younker Reporter*. "The amount each employee saves is entirely voluntary, for it is the regular setting aside of a certain amount that counts."[64]

Page 4   THE YOUNKER REPORTER

Captains and Veteran Captains in Victory Loan Drive

The captains and veteran captains for the five Younker armies are shown above as they appeared at the kick-off rally in the Tea Room Thursday morning, October 25. They are, left to right, top row: Captains Wm. Bennett, Cliff Lackey, Hans Holmes, John Lane and Dave Levich. Front row: Veteran Captains Howard Cox, Sam Rizzuti, Robert Cramer, Ollie Silverstein and Eddie Johnson.

For the last of eight war bond drives, employees divided into five teams named for the U.S. field armies. *CB.*

Four months later, participation was at nearly 97 percent, but the dollar amount being purchased was too low to suit the federal government, and the secretary of the treasury asked that the per capita allotment be raised to 10 percent of income. In the June 1942 *Younker Reporter*, the editor railed at employees, "Don't say you can't afford to keep on buying bonds, just as though that's all there is to it! Maybe the 44 men from Younkers, and the hundreds of thousands of American boys overseas 'couldn't afford to go to war'—but they've gone, and they're fighting for you and me…This is a fight to the finish. This is a battle that we've all got to fight. America needs us…our men, our machines, our energies, our abilities, our ingenuity… our DOLLARS!"[65]

Younkers converted a display window on the Walnut Street side of the store to a Bond Shelter, with an entrance through a door marked, "Doorway to Freedom." Auxiliary members of the American Legion staffed the window for two weeks. Thereafter, employees, assisted by about eight hundred female volunteers recruited by the Polk County Volunteers Committee, sold bonds and stamps from a booth on the first floor east. Stamps could also be bought at the post office branch on the second floor.[66]

Between employee purchases, payroll deduction and sales to customers, the store surpassed not only its quota of $25,000 but also the $274,000 quota set for all of Des Moines and Polk County. Benjamin Namm, the chairman of the Retail Advisory Committee for the U.S. Treasury War Savings Staff, wrote to applaud the company for its outstanding success and added, "We hope that you realize that July marks the beginning rather than the end of 'Retailers for Victory.' We are counting upon a continuance of your splendid support under the leadership of your great chief, Mr. Henry Frankel." *Women's Wear Daily* even took note of the achievement in its August 12, 1942 edition, writing, "Younkers is believed to have oversold its quota by a larger margin than any other department store in the country."[67]

Frankel assured employees that management was indeed committed to the bond campaigns over selling merchandise. His message before the annual Capacity Day sale on June 3, 1942, stated:

Even more important than selling Capacity Day is the selling of War Savings stamps and bonds. It is the patriotic privilege of those of us who are not asked into the front line trenches, to do everything possible to supply the ammunition to those on the firing line…. Surely no one needs to be timid about asking customers if they will take some of their change in War Savings stamps. No one need be afraid of offending a customer, because any

Victory Loan Message by Co-Chairmen

TOTAL VICTORY is now ours. But, we still have a big job ahead of us,—to bring home millions of our boys from overseas. The home front cannot and will not give up until it has the assurance of security and a worry-free future. With the Five Legion Armies all fighting for top places each week, competition is running high with enthusiasm, as well as bond sales. We know Younkers will do the job well! It's up to us to put this all important Victory Loan over the top. "They finished their job . . . Let's finish ours!!"

Mable Kutch   Ruth McGlothlen

Women chaired or co-chaired at least two of the store's eight bond campaigns. *CB.*

customer who will take offense at such an approach would be assuming an unpatriotic attitude. Our duty today, to our 44 boys who are in war service, is to sell, and buy, War Savings stamps and bonds in Capacity quantities. No one of our loyal organization will fail to do so.[68]

Payroll deductions and store sales weren't enough to finance the war, however, so the Treasury Department introduced the "drive" system, with themes and sales goals. Between November 1942 and May 1945, the Treasury Department launched seven bond drives. The first two set no quotas. Beginning with the third, retail workers were expected to sell a minimum of $200 each in bonds, later increasing to $300. For every campaign, Younkers not only met the quota but surpassed it, often by dramatic margins.

To encourage the community to buy, the store devoted its two blocks of display windows to the war bond drives. For the third drive, images from Walt Disney's animated film *Victory Through Air Power* provided lively visuals, and an airplane engine, army outfits and displays of official medals and decorations attracted passersby. Inside the store, customers could ring a replica of the Liberty Bell when they bought a bond. Zola Palmer, manager of the basement music department, played patriotic tunes on the Hammond electric organ every morning and at noon, and the short film *Women at War*, featuring the Women's Army Corps training camp at Fort Des Moines, was

Portraits of World War II leaders painted by staff artist George Rackelmann filled display windows for one drive. In 1985, they were donated to the State Historical Society. *MR.*

aired. For another drive, Younkers was one of a few department stores in the country to host a traveling exhibition of German tanks, planes, guns and equipment captured in North Africa. Arranged along Eighth Street for a week in January, the display drew large and curious crowds.[69]

Over a three-and-a-half-year period, Younkers employees sold a whopping $14,369,795 in bonds and war stamps. That included $550,875 in E bonds bought through payroll deduction and another $416,500 that employees and their families purchased at the bond booth. Beyond that figure, the company itself bought $40,000 in bonds to give to employees as Christmas gifts. Des Moines retailers as a group were assigned a total quota of $9,700,000 for E bond sales; Younkers alone sold nearly 43 percent of the quota.[70]

In addition to throwing enormous amounts of energy and resources into the war bond drives, Younkers helped publicize the drives nationwide with a series of "war stamp dresses." The first dress, designed and sewn by the alterations department under the direction of Sadie Byrd, went to Hollywood in January 1943 at the request of the United States Treasury Department. There, it was modeled at a bond rally by Canadian-born actress Alexis Smith, who had just appeared with Errol Flynn in *Gentleman Jim* (1942). Photographs of the star in the stamp dress appeared in three movie magazines. It was replaced with a second gown that incorporated $1,500 in stamps and bonds and went on tour with the 1944 Maid of

Cotton, Linwood Gisclard, who donned the dress to promote bond sales at fifty major retail stores across the South and Midwest. Byrd and her team produced a third and fourth dress to continue touring and promoting bond sales at events large and small through 1945.[71]

YOUNKERITES IN SERVICE

Like every organization and every family, Younkers had a personal investment in the war. Between December 1941 and May 1945, 217 employees (about 18 percent of the workforce) enlisted in one of the services. Most were in the army, but the navy, marines, merchant marine and Coast Guard were also represented, as well as WACs, WAVES and U.S. Coast Guard Women's Reserve. As did department stores across the country, Younkers posted an honor roll with the names of all its men and women enlisted in the various branches. Two men and one woman died while in service. One was Norman W. Mandelbaum, brother of Morris Mandelbaum Jr. and son of a director and vice-president of the company. In addition, many employees lost family members.[72]

WELCOMING THE WACS

In addition to supporting the war through bond drives, Younkers also played a unique role in helping the U.S. Army outfit the first three groups of the Women's Army Auxiliary Corps (WAACs) that came to Fort Des Moines for training. Established in 1942, the WAACs (renamed Women's Army Corps in 1943) recruited and trained women for support roles ranging from switchboard operators to mechanics, bakers, drivers and secretaries. Basic job and fitness training took place at Fort Des Moines at the Provisional Army Officer Training School, starting in July 1942.[73]

Younkers' staff had about three weeks to prepare, organizing space at the fort for processing, fitting and tailoring all clothing that would be issued to the recruits. To handle the project, the store brought in twenty-five electric sewing machines and four specialty machines for hemming, basting, hemstitching and zipper installation. Ironing boards and irons, steam irons and sewing machines for corsets and bras were also acquired.[74]

Younkers outfitted the Women's Army Auxiliary Corps recruits who came to be trained at Fort Des Moines, 1942.

Golda Cole from the gloves department described the experience: "We Younker people met at the store corner of Seventh and Walnut at 6:30 in the morning and rode the street car out to the end of the line where we were met by soldiers in army trucks. From there we were driven to the processing building to work." After being checked in and given passes, they took their stations:

> At 7:30 we started running through groups of the WAACs...Each woman was given a duffle bag and a list of government issue garments to be measured and furnished. First the new WAACs were measured for girdles and bras, and then individually taken to one of the eight fitting rooms for a try-on. Next in line, measurements were taken for hats, gloves, slips, robes, pajamas, shirts, skirts, coats, and then shoes. At the end of the line each item was verified. Then the WAACs filed through the supply room where each was issued the right size clothing. Finally they arrived at the alteration room where our fitters checked and made the necessary alterations.[75]

The store welcomed the female recruits with a booklet describing all the services available at Younkers. Most were the standard services offered to all customers, but the booklet's illustrations and text targeted the new women officers and auxiliaries. The War Bond Booth and stocking repair shop, both on first floor east, spoke directly to the wartime situation, with the latter particularly pertinent for the women. "Bring your rayon and cotton stockings to our new Repair Shop and our wonderful new service will rescue them for still more wear. You'll be surprised at how little it will cost to save them. Silk and Nylon stockings repaired, also."[76]

Much of America was not ready for women in the military, however, and a national slander campaign was unleashed in 1943 by hostile enlisted men and religious and social conservatives.[77] Perhaps as part of an effort to counter any negative publicity locally, the Des Moines WAC recruiting office partnered with Younkers in September 1944 to open a WAColony Club lounge on the fifth floor east. Here members of the public could enjoy a free Coca-Cola, watch movies and chat with members of the Women's Army Corps. During the first six weeks, more than 2,500 visitors stopped by. Lieutenant Elizabeth G. Berryhill, the officer in charge of the Des Moines recruiting station, said that the club "has given us a chance to meet civilian women informally and to thank them for their many courtesies to all members of the armed services." The club was deemed so successful that Killian's department store in Cedar Rapids decided to open its own version, called the biv-WAC.[78]

BUSINESS NOT QUITE AS USUAL

Although store management promoted support of the war effort over profits, Younkers still had to do business—to continue providing customers with the goods they had always come to the store to buy. Through 1942 and 1943, rationing and shortages of materials diverted to wartime production meant that the name brands, quality and variety of merchandise that Younkers could offer before the war were no longer available. Staffing also suffered, as men and women joined the military and were not replaced. Deliveries had to be cut back, and the quality of service declined.[79]

To compensate for these shortages, the store rearranged and redecorated departments. It made the most of the merchandise it had by presenting moderately priced clothing, hats and shoes in a series of Fashion Street

Shops on the main floor of the west building. Staff carpenters and painters redecorated the area in a mulberry-and-turquoise color scheme and added seven new "elaborately decorated fitting rooms" to give the redesigned area a feeling of richness that played down the mid-level quality of the goods. Linens, domestics and toys all found new locations, and the mail-order service was streamlined in response to increased demand.[80]

With European goods hard to get, Younkers went south of the border for new items, introducing a South American Shop on the fourth floor west. The decorative accessories and giftware were actually from Mexico, Haiti and Guatemala rather than South America, but more merchandise was expected "in real quantities for one of the most colorful spots in the store."[81] The California shop, with pottery and home decorating accessories, formed a new special section of the gift shop on fourth floor west.

THE BATTLE OF THE BULGE

With the war entering its fourth year, the United States Congress issued a request that "all Americans join in Bible reading," to seek divine help with "the problems that face our country and all humanity in these crucial days, from now until victory." As it had with the bond sale campaigns, Younkers readily complied. On January 25, 1945 (ironically, the last day of the Battle of the Bulge), Younkers dedicated a full page of advertising space in the *Des Moines Register* to the message, "Read Your Bible, America." Titled "A New World Dawns When You Start Reading Your Bible," the advertisement addressed all Americans but particularly "mothers and wives at home," encouraging them to turn to the Bible for comfort and courage. The company was pleasantly surprised by the public's enthusiastic response to the message. It received more than one hundred letters the week after the ad's appearance and requests from other stores to republish the same ad in their own hometowns.[82]

While Victory in Europe was greeted with relief, Japan's surrender on August 15, 1945, was buried inside the *Younker Reporter* published two days later. "Younkerites put in two nervous days of anxious waiting this week before the Japanese surrender news came Tuesday evening," the newsletter reported. "The store had closed at 5:30, and when the radio flash came at 6 o'clock, most of the employees were on their way home." Only restaurant guests remained in the store, along with Tea Room and

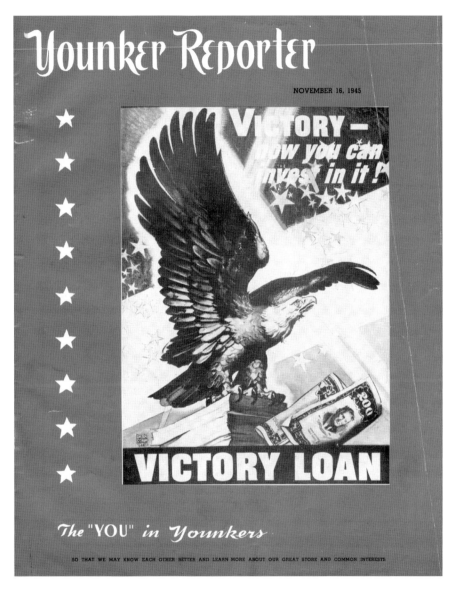

The Victory Loan Drive, from October 29 to December 8, 1945, marked the end of the bond campaigns to finance the war. *CB.*

Cremona Room staff. "Customers in the buffet hearing the excitement looked out the windows of the north serving room in time to see the first shower of paper fluttering down from the Register and Tribune building." Downtown streets filled with people celebrating, and eighteen guards gathered around the store to keep the plate glass windows from being damaged. The store's window dressers had clearly been anticipating the victory celebrations, as "curtains on all show windows were quickly drawn behind huge flags of the United Nations hung next to the glass. A single flag hung in each window on the two-block front."[83]

More than twenty-five thousand people, mostly young, sang and danced in the streets, causing streetcars, buses and taxis to suspend service for four hours. Thousands of cars descended on downtown and clogged the loop. Younkers had originally planned on a one-day victory holiday, but President Truman and Iowa's Governor Blue declared both Wednesday and Thursday holidays for state and federal employees. Younkers followed suit.

The End of Rationing

As rationing lifted for consumer goods, the greatest danger of a customer feeding frenzy came from an apparently innocuous quarter: nylon stockings. Younkers sought to impose order and fairness on sales with a decision to sell nylons only by mail order on a first-come, first-served basis. Instead of releasing the scarce stockings as supplies trickled in, the store set them aside. In an advertisement in the city edition of the *Des Moines Register* on Thursday morning, February 21, 1946, Younkers acknowledged the dismay this must have caused: "We've been criticized, we know, for holding precious NYLONS, but we think this fair plan of distribution will vindicate us." To buy a single pair of stockings, women had to mail in a postcard or letter with their name, address and size and whether they had a charge account. All requests had to be postmarked by midnight Saturday, February 23. Customers were instructed to send no money and not to call or come by the store. Stockings would be delivered to charge customers, and cash customers would be notified by mail when and where to pick up their purchase. Rayon stockings were being discontinued because of diminishing supplies, but any customer who preferred them to nylon could receive two pair instead of one pair of nylons.[84]

Within hours of the ad's appearance, penny postcards flooded the post office. By 11:00 a.m., the store had received about one thousand of them. Although the ad only appeared in the Des Moines edition, a letter arrived Saturday morning from Michigan. "There were outcroppings of attempted 'chiseling' usual in such mass movements," noted the *Younker Reporter*, but the divisional merchandise manager "devised an identification system whereby positive identity would be required of those customers who were asked to call at the store for their hose. Driver's licenses, social security cards, liquor books were named as identifying agents."

Younkers devised its mail-order plan after studying what stores in other large cities had done. "Wherever Nylons were offered over the counter the crowds became unmanageable," explained the *Younker Reporter*. "Neither was the distribution fair, because many persons got double lots and some persons could not attend, or would not get in the crowds to be mauled and pushed."

Management rewarded its employees for their loyalty and

Women Have Been Waiting for

NYLON STOCKINGS!

so here's our PLAN!

WE'VE been criticized, we know, for holding precious NYLONS. but we think this fair plan of distribution will vindicate us. It has been a perplexing problem. We want to avoid crowds, tiresome waiting, confusion and disappointments. We do want to take care of our charge and cash customers equitably. We have accumulated a quantity of pairs by saving small shipments trickling in each week. Not a pair has been sold or given to anyone. If you're interested (and we suspect you are) please read our plan carefully.

Registration by MAIL ONLY by WOMEN ONLY!

To avoid chaotic competition for scarce nylon stockings, Younkers devised a mail-order purchase plan.

hard work with an advance sale of the precious commodity. All Younkerites received a coupon in their pay envelopes on February 19, "entitling them to purchase one pair of Nylons at an advance sale for employees only." Distribution was alphabetical.

In the fall of 1944, the Younkers leadership was already looking ahead to the end of the war, hoping that victory in Europe might allow Younkers to resume its plans for growth. In addition, a new concept in furniture sales was in the planning stages. Younkers was ready—and already taking steps—to break new ground in retailing in Iowa.

Chapter 6

MIDCENTURY EXPANSION

Ordinarily, Younkers adopted a considered approach to change, learning from the experiences of other department stores. When it came to branch stores, however, the company took the lead. By the time other major department stores around the country began opening branches in the late 1940s and early 1950s, Younkers already had six stores up and running.[85] The Little Shop opened in Ames in 1941, followed over the next eight years by stores in Mason City, Fort Dodge, Ottumwa, Marshalltown and Iowa City.

The decision to grow by planting branch stores drew on Younkers' charge-account data. It showed that customers came from all over the state to make their major purchases at the Des Moines store. In addition, as branch operations manager Jack Zavatsky explained, movies, radio, magazines and cars were all contributing to a more homogenized society. Men and women wanted stylish clothing, home furnishings and conveniences regardless of whether they lived in town or in the country. Management reasoned that making Younkers' quality and service available in smaller towns would boost overall sales and win new customers for the flagship store, which would offer the bigger items that the branches couldn't carry.[86] Henry Frankel was credited with launching the branch strategy, but it developed into a well-organized system under his successor as president, Morey Sostrin, and chairman of the board Joseph Rosenfield.

FROM DOWNTOWN TO YOUR TOWN

Like the flagship store, all of the early branches were in downtown commercial centers. In several cases, Younkers entered an already-crowded market and bought out older, locally owned competitors, using their buildings until it could construct its own. Beginning with the second branch store in Mason City, Younkers used its own staff architect, Omar Franklin, to oversee renovations and installation of store fixtures.

With the Fort Dodge store in 1947, Younkers executives introduced the practice of preceding branch openings with a lunch for local business leaders, city officials and members of civic groups. Sostrin would spell out the Younkers philosophy and seek to allay fears of disruptive competition. In Fort Dodge, he told the assembly, "We are not coming to Fort Dodge with 'big shot' or 'big city' ideas. We are considered home town folks in Des Moines, Ames and Mason City and we intend to be just that here." He assured them that Younkers had no interest in stealing employees or vendors from other companies, which might mean that brands carried in Des Moines

The Mason City branch store opened to enthusiastic crowds in 1944. *SHSI.*

would not be offered in Fort Dodge if another store carried them. "In no case will we ask a manufacturer to drop a Fort Dodge customer to favor us," he said.[87] The gesture earned good will and cemented the store's reputation for fair dealing with both customers and competitors.

GROWTH THROUGH SUBSIDIARIES

In Sioux City, Younkers took a different approach. Davidson's, founded by two immigrant brothers in 1884, was a large and well-respected department store with 450 employees, many of whom had worked there for up to thirty years. In 1948, Younkers bought the department store and kept most of the employees as well as the name, hyphenating it with the Younker name. Rather than being part of the branch system, Younker-Davidson's was run as a wholly owned subsidiary of Younker Brothers Inc., with its own buyers and advertising department.[88] Later, when Younkers bought the nearby T.S. Martin department store, it put the Younker-Davidson's management in charge and kept both stores in operation until 1969, when urban renewal plans forced the closing of Younker-Martin's.

Younker Brothers Inc. also sought expansion farther afield with purchases in Kansas and Colorado. In 1952, the company bought the largest department store in Kansas, Wichita's George Innes Company, with the intention of operating it as an independent subsidiary. In 1954, Younkers joined forces with Boston Store Dry Goods of Fort Smith, Arkansas, to buy a controlling interest in Daniel & Fisher of Denver, a huge downtown store and a community institution. Within a few years, Younkers had pulled out of both in order to invest in suburban development closer to home. It sold the Innes Company to Macy's in 1956 and its interest in Daniel & Fisher to May Department Stores Company in 1957.[89]

OUT TO THE 'BURBS

Suburban shopping centers with integrated parking dated back to the 1920s and 1930s but were usually built in densely populated areas. By the 1950s, with the postwar housing boom, even midsize towns were beginning to spread out into the countryside as housing developments cropped up in former cornfields. Shopping centers quickly followed. Whether the centers were simply strips offering services and convenience shopping or larger complexes anchored by major department stores, they were a radical departure from the downtown commercial districts.

Developed, owned and managed by a single company that leased space to tenants and maintained the property, suburban shopping centers reflected the changing patterns of residential development and America's growing love affair with the car. They also represented a cultural shift in the way people shopped and spent their leisure time. As Morey Sostrin explained, it wasn't just a matter of people living farther and farther from the city center that made shopping centers more convenient. The acres of free parking were an enticement, as was the fact that people could simply "hop in their cars, dressed in house dresses and slacks—or even shorts, accompanied by their families, to go shopping together," he wrote.[90] Shopping at the downtown Des Moines store, on the other hand, was still a special event in the 1950s, and women dressed up for it, complete with hat, gloves and matching shoes and bag.

Younkers' first venture into suburbia took the company to Omaha. Developer John A. Wiebe thought that his hometown looked like a good bet for Nebraska's first regional shopping center—a development distinguished from convenience shopping centers by its larger size, layout and dependence on large department stores as anchors. He approached Younkers about anchoring the new mall, located three miles from downtown. The Center opened in 1955 with about thirty stores on three levels and parking decks at each level. A bowling alley occupied the floor above Younkers, which took up more than half of the mall's 195,000 square feet of shopping space.[91] (In 1961, the store was renamed and put under the management of Younkers' newly acquired, wholly owned Omaha subsidiary, Kilpatrick's. In early 1968, Kilpatrick's opened a large, upscale suburban store at Westroads Mall, which at 1,150,000 square feet was one of the largest malls in America.)[92]

The company's next venture into suburbia came in 1956, when Younkers signed a deal with Chicago developer Bernard Greenbaum & Associates to anchor what would become Merle Hay Shopping Plaza in northwest Des Moines. Merle Hay was the first regional shopping center in the state. When the store opened in August 1959, Sostrin acknowledged that it would probably take some business from the downtown store, but officials hoped that the two stores together would produce better results than one alone.[93] As it turned out, the Merle Hay store became one of the most important and productive in the chain.

After Merle Hay, Younkers continued opening branch stores in large and small shopping centers and malls across Iowa and into Minnesota, Illinois and South Dakota. It also experimented with different merchandising models to compete with changes in the retail environment.

SELF-SERVICE AT EASTGATE

Whether you shopped Younkers downtown or at a branch store, you could expect the same attentive service. Friendly, helpful associates committed to "Satisfaction Always" were the hallmark of Younkers stores, no matter where they were located. But that service was relatively costly, and as discount stores and mass merchants increasingly won shoppers away from department stores, Younkers looked for new ways to compete.

In October 1962, the company opened its first self-service store, Younkers-East (later known as Eastgate), at East Fourteenth Street and Euclid in Des Moines. The idea was to reduce operating costs by adopting some of the features of supermarkets—such as minimal service and speedy front-of-store checkout—while pursuing "added sales on a price and value basis… This, again, is an indication of our thinking in meeting current trends in retail distribution," Sostrin explained to employees.[94] Sostrin noted that the single-level unit had abundant free parking and carried the same nationally advertised brands as the flagship store, merchandise not available to discount stores. The company had adopted a policy three years earlier of "meeting

The 1944 downtown Mason City branch was replaced with a fifty-thousand-square-foot store in 1984. *MR.*

any price in town on identical goods in addition to our long-time policy of credit and delivery," he added. (The policy of "we will not knowingly be undersold" remained in place until 1981.)

In another departure from Younkers' tradition, the store would be open on Sundays, a competitive necessity that Sostrin deplored. (The Merle Hay and downtown stores remained closed on Sundays until 1970, when Younkers succumbed to peer pressure and began opening the Merle Hay store on Sundays from noon to 5:30 p.m.)[95]

In the summer of 1964, the *Younker Reporter* announced that for the first time, sales volume in the branches exceeded the volume at the main store. The Ames branch was the most productive, churning out "more volume per square foot of floor space than any other Younker branch store," according to Sostrin. However, the newsletter pointed out that the flagship store still produced one-third of the corporation's total business and was in the process of being completely renovated—an indication of the company's continuing commitment to downtown Des Moines.[96]

DEALING WITH DISASTER

Fires large and small were always a hazard for retail establishments, whether the store was downtown or in a shopping center. Younkers lost personnel records and a considerable amount of merchandise when the building on Seventh and Locust Streets, where it rented two floors, caught fire in January 1962. (The replacement for this building, the Parkade, combined a public parking garage and new retail space for Younkers.) On October 17, 1969, the branch store at the Center in Omaha suffered major damage when a fire started in the bowling alley above it. Then, just a month later on November 20, 1969, the downtown Tea Room ceiling was damaged when accumulated grease in the exhaust fan caught fire around 2:00 p.m. Late-lunch diners left reluctantly when smoke began pouring into the restaurants, and the blaze caused several thousand dollars in damage.[97]

The worst disaster, however, occurred at the Merle Hay store on Sunday, November 5, 1978. An explosion and subsequent fire at about 9:30 a.m. left ten employees dead and destroyed the main section of the store. An official with the National Fire Prevention Association called the store fire "one of the worst in the nation." The reinforced-concrete structure, which had originally been touted as fireproof, had no sprinkler system because its construction predated fire code requirements for one. The Younkers budget store and Store for Homes and the rest of the mall were undamaged.[98]

The investigation into the cause produced the theory that hydrogen gas formed when alkaline water leaking from the cooling system dripped onto aluminum cooling fins and aluminum-coated insulation. The gas, highly flammable but odorless, apparently built up until a spark of unknown origin ignited it.[99] Litigation dragged on for years; Younkers refused to admit that it was guilty of safety violations and ultimately paid a small fine levied by the Iowa Occupational Safety and Health Review Commission.[100]

Both Younkers and the estates of the victims launched a volley of suits against about twenty companies connected with the polyvinyl coating on the wiring, believed to have contributed to the explosion. In 1984, a jury found for the plaintiffs, and the defendants, including Monsanto and Underwriters Laboratories, settled the lawsuit (the amounts remained confidential).[101]

While lawyers and city and state officials debated, Younkers proceeded to rebuild the ruined store. Less than a year after the fire, the new store opened with little fanfare. "Under the circumstances, it would have been inappropriate to have a 'grand opening' or a festive kind of thing," company president William Friedman Jr. told the *Des Moines Register*. The new store surpassed "all fire code, worker safety and insurance standards," according to the newspaper. Store executives emphasized all the new safety features—sprinkler system, smoke detectors, computerized fire detection, fire alarms everywhere and seven emergency stairways. Younkers also established trust funds for the minor children of the fire's victims to provide for their education.[102]

THE AUTOMOTIVE BUSINESS

Along with establishing branches in downtown commercial districts and in suburban shopping centers, Younkers saw an opportunity in the growing dependence on automobiles. The store had sold tires in 1937, but the redirection of rubber to the war effort eliminated that item from its inventory. More than twenty years later, the company ventured back into the tire and auto supply business. While at first glance surprising, the investment actually obeyed the same logic that drove the emerging expansion into suburbia, an acknowledgement of the supremacy of car culture in America. Through a licensing deal with Abel Corporation in 1960, the company gained access to expertise and merchandise that were otherwise outside its realm.

Although downtown workers might live in the suburbs, car dealerships and repair shops still clustered near the city center in Des Moines. The new Younker Tire Center, located at Ninth Street and Grand Avenue, was just three blocks from the flagship store, within easy walking distance, so customers could drop off their cars and go shopping. The tire center offered Abel Label tires, batteries, seat covers and auto supplies, as well as nationally advertised brands.[103] Younkers added a second Younkers Tire Center four years later.

In 1946, *Fashion Trades Weekly* had described Younkers as "the 'Grass Roots' merchandising leviathan of Iowa.... Younkers of Iowa sells everything to all of Iowa. The store is a state institution."[104] By 1950, Younkers was among the one hundred largest retailers in the nation in terms of 1948 dollar sales. Twenty-three years later, thanks to its strategy of growth through branches, Younkers was a major midwestern chain, with twenty-two stores and more than $100 million in sales.[105] And in spite of a bumpy economy in the 1970s and 1980s, it kept on growing.

Chapter 7

THE YOUNKERS TEA ROOM

Of all the things people remember about the Younkers' downtown flagship store, the Tea Room evokes the fondest memories. It became legendary as a stately, gracious place for lunch or dinner, a "first fancy dining experience" for children and the best way to impress a first date.

Author Bill Bryson, who grew up in Des Moines, paid tribute to the Tea Room in his memoir, *The Life and Times of the Thunderbolt Kid*: "The Tea Room was the most elegant place I had ever been—like a stateroom from Buckingham Palace magically transported to the Middle West of America."[106]

By the time the Younkers Tea Room opened in 1913, the idea of incorporating a restaurant into a department store had become the norm across the country. Macy's and Wanamaker's offered food service as early as the 1870s as a convenience for female shoppers, who couldn't go into a restaurant unescorted without risking social embarrassment. This early food service earned low marks, however, and usually consisted of cold food prepared off-site. In 1890, Harry Selfridge, the visionary store manager at Marshall Field, showed how successful an upscale tearoom could be. By 1903, his store's tearoom was serving three thousand people per day.[107]

Although Aaron Younker moved to Chicago in 1908, he continued serving as vice-president of Younkers, so it seems more than possible that he saw Selfridge's success at Marshall Field and encouraged Younkers to offer the same service. The news of the plan was greeted with skepticism, however. When the manager of the Des Moines Club shared with a fellow restaurant

REFLECTIONS IN *Younkers* TEA ROOM
DES MOINES, IOWA

Where you meet your friends and enjoy good food

Decorated in elegant Georgian style, the Younkers Tea Room hosted fashion shows, dinner dances, banquets and meetings. *JC.*

owner that Younkers was opening a tearoom like the one in Chicago, the two agreed, "It won't work, no sir, it won't work!"[108]

They were quite wrong. Installed on the sixth floor of the original (east) building, the Younkers Tea Room quickly became a popular meeting place for business luncheons, banquets, bridge clubs and women's groups. Harris-Emery, not to be outdone, also had tearooms that hosted similar meetings and functions. When Younkers acquired the Wilkins Building in 1924, it moved the restaurant to that building's fifth floor and invested in larger, more elaborately decorated facilities, aiming for an edge over its competitors.

An Iowa Institution

The new Tea Room and auxiliary dining rooms debuted late in 1925. When the elevator doors opened, hungry patrons found themselves in an exotic Spanish-style alameda (or public space) and lounge, decorated with Spanish lanterns, hand-woven tapestries, antique Spanish chests bound with iron and chairs with hand-tooled leather seats.

In the main tearoom, glittering crystal chandeliers illuminated a large, elegant space divided by tall, square columns and ornamented with Georgian-style details. A velvet-curtained stage with orchestra pit and dance floor anchored one end of the room, which could seat about 350 people.

Two smaller rooms, equally formal, accommodated club luncheons, bridge parties and meetings. One, decorated in an Adamesque scheme of blue and gold with antique satin hangings in gold and black, could hold two hundred people. "For the more formal and exclusive dinners and luncheons, the French room will afford a handsome Louis XV setting," noted the 1926 employee bulletin. No expense had been spared on this room: gold leaf highlighted the plaster relief moldings, and crystal light fixtures sparkled against French ivory walls and ceiling. Chairs were upholstered in an imported, custom-designed satin, and ornamental paneled mirrors hung on the walls.

There were also three private rooms decorated in a "truly American," modern style with dull green- and blue-glazed woodwork and panels with red lacquer stripes. The rooms could be closed off for small groups or opened up to create one large dining room.[109]

From the 1920s through the Depression and World War II, patrons came to the Tea Room to enjoy a leisurely lunch or dinner and weekly lunchtime

The 1925 Tea Room foyer was decorated in Spanish style. *JC.*

Three private dining rooms, decorated in "American" style, opened off the main Tea Room. *JC.*

fashion shows while a professional musician played the piano or organ in the background. The most famous Tea Room musician was Louis Weertz, better known as Roger Williams. The son of the Reverend Frederick J. Weertz, pastor of St. John's Lutheran Church downtown, Williams started playing piano at age three and studied at Drake University and Juilliard. He went on to become an enormously successful pianist with Billboard hits such as "Autumn Leaves," "Born Free" and themes from the movies *Dr. Zhivago* and *Somewhere in Time*.[110] In November 1931, Doc Lawson, a locally famous theater organist, brought his nine-piece orchestra to perform in the Tea Room daily during the lunch hour as well as for dinner dances, the College Club dances on Friday nights and late-night dancing on Saturdays.[111]

The Tea Room and adjoining dining rooms hosted fine-arts lectures, book review clubs, private parties and cooking schools, as well as annual holiday parties and monthly dinner meetings of businesses and professional organizations. Every year, children flocked to the Tea Room for Easter and Halloween parties. The *Des Moines Register and Tribune* rented the space for an annual dinner honoring students competing in its spelling bee. Campfire Girls held its annual Father-Daughter banquet here, and the Girl Scouts reserved the Tea Room for its yearly dinner. The Des Moines National Bank took over the space for its annual Christmas party, which required the kitchen staff to cook twenty-four turkeys, one for each table. Members of 4-H were

The store's holiday party for employees in 1945 included a sit-down dinner in the Tea Room and the adjacent dining rooms. *CB.*

Every March, the Iowa Girls Athletic Association held its banquet in the Tea Room. *IGAA.*

honored during the state fair, graduation and school banquets were held here and athletes participating in the girls' state basketball tournament filled the room for breakfast every March.

By 1949, the *Younker Reporter* could boast that the Tea Room was held in such high esteem, not only in Des Moines but throughout Iowa, "that it has become almost as famous as the department store of which it is a part. It is accepted as an institution in the city's life."[112]

"REALLY GOOD FOOD"

For many department stores, a well-regarded restaurant boosted the store's overall prestige. In fact, so many department stores invested in good-quality restaurants that they constituted one of the largest categories in guidebooks for travelers.[113] Younkers was included in AAA listings and in Duncan Hines's *Adventures in Good Eating*, which described the Tea Room as "nationally known for really good food." It mentioned among the specialties the fried chicken, cinnamon rolls, pastries, steaks and salads.[114] In 1962, the Duncan Hines Institute awarded the Tea Room a silver anniversary service award for having merited inclusion in Hines's book for twenty-five years.

Among locals, the Tea Room was famous for its "white meat of chicken salad," homemade salad dressings, cinnamon rolls, burnt almond sponge and Boston clam chowder. Tea Room manager George Whinery modified the menu from time to time in response to consumer trends. In 1960, the "Bountiful Buffet" introduced an all-you-can-eat lunch buffet offering "gourmet foods, five or six kinds of salads as well as hot and cold vegetables and appetizers" that Whinery compared to "raiding the icebox at home, and exercising the right of individual choice to suit their own taste." Even dieters, he said, could benefit from the buffet.

"In the restaurant business, we have to cater to all kinds of eating habits," he noted. "We serve a luncheon salad with low calorie dressing, rye krisp and black coffee to the dieters or the breakfast-plus-coffee break eaters. We have full meals for the thousands who can eat whatever they like without affecting their weight, or for those who are trying to gain weight." Although he admitted that Americans were modifying their diets in response to health concerns, he pointed out that hefty meals were still popular. The Tea Room menu had just added a French picnic luncheon loaf, "a mansize sandwich filled with meats, cheese, hard cooked eggs, tomato, cucumber, onion rings and head lettuce." You could also order pancakes and waffles every day—blueberry, buckwheat, wheat, pecan and brunch waffles were always available.[115]

The Tea Room made a point of appealing to children, serving them on their own china from menus geared to children's tastes. The restaurant even provided bibs for the toddlers. The best part came after the meal, when the waitress would bring the "Treasure Chest," from which young patrons could choose a gift. The "treasures" were usually little more than trinkets, but wrapped in white tissue paper and tied with a pink or blue ribbon, they seemed special and exciting.

Periodic redecorating updated the rooms according to current tastes. In 1936, the party rooms adjacent to the Tea Room were done over in Wedgwood blue and ivory, and new lighting fixtures were installed. In the fall of 1952 and the winter of 1953, the foyer underwent a radical makeover in the name of modernization. A dropped ceiling of acoustical tiles and semi-recessed lights focused attention down toward the low, streamlined wood and vinyl seating, the "modernistic display cases and ornamental driftwood bracket lights." Folding "leatherette" doors led to the main dining room beyond.[116]

LET'S MEET FOR LUNCH AT YOUNKERS

When Younkers moved the Tea Room to the new west building in 1925, it also opened the Cremona Room in the basement. Shoppers, office workers and employees all patronized this luncheonette, which served continuously from 11:00 a.m. to 7:30 pm., offering affordable dinner and lunch items, salads, sandwiches and soda fountain treats. After the store closed at 5:30 p.m., you could enter directly through the south door on Eighth Street. In the 1940s, the Cremona Room served about 2,500 at lunch and dinner and another 800 at the soda fountain daily. By 1964, however, tastes had changed, and it was replaced with a new coffeehouse more in tune with the times.[117]

With the Tea Room for elegant, leisurely dining and the Cremona Room for budget meals and snacks, in 1940 Younkers offered yet another option: the Garden Buffet, targeting downtown office workers and professionals with an eye on the clock. It offered a greater variety of hot and cold foods than the Tea Room, with the convenience of cafeteria service and lower prices. Apparently, men had felt excluded from the main Tea Room because the *Younker Reporter* noted that "men as well as women are now welcomed." The Tea Room kitchen prepared the food and transported it to the buffet in closed carts.[118]

Nearly twenty years later, Younkers responded to changing eating habits by replacing the Garden Buffet with the Rose Room. Still targeting the office worker on a lunch break or the Saturday shopper, the Rose Room offered moderately priced meals and fountain service in a casual setting. The Tea Room menu was upgraded to offer "more luxurious meals" at slightly higher prices to maintain its status as the premier dining spot in the store.[119]

Unlike the Garden Buffet, the Rose Room had its own kitchen and dishwashing equipment and thus its own cook and kitchen staff. Formica tabletops and counters paired with light, golden paneling and midcentury modern cane-back chairs gave the restaurant a modern, informal look. A

A Corner of the Garden Room
YOUNKERS TEA ROOM
Des Moines, Iowa

VALENTINE MENU

Oyster Sampler Plate: Mignonette (Shallots, Olive Oil and Sherry Vinegar)
Rockefeller (Spinach, Bacon, Shallots, Cream and Pernod)
Fritters (Fried Oysters) $7.25

Salad: Splendid Raspberry Spinach Salad
(Spinach tossed with Raspberry Vinaigrette, Raspberries,
Kiwi and Toasted Almonds.)

Entrees: Steak Diane $16.95
Shrimp Scampi $18.25
Blackened Scallops $15.50

(All include salad, starch, vegetable and dessert)

Starch: Quenelles of Horseradish Whipped Potatoes

Vegetable: Asparagus with Hot Bacon Dressing

Dessert: Chocolate Sin-sation with Berry Sauce

Above, left: The Garden Room offered downtown office workers convenient cafeteria-style service. *JC.*

Above, right: The Rose Room targeted the office worker and Saturday shopper, but the Valentine's Day menu seems fairly upscale. *CB.*

Left: The Rose Room's Syracuse china was a popular choice for restaurants in the Midwest. *CB.*

large window overlooked the Des Moines skyline to the north. On the east and west walls, hand-painted murals by Dwight Kirsch, former director of the Des Moines Art Center and a well-known midwestern artist, depicted a weathered fence, wild roses (Iowa's state flower) and mail boxes, with farm buildings in the distance. The murals were flecked with gold leaf, "and the entire concept of color is delicate and lyrical," according to the *Des Moines Register*'s George Shane. The china, by Syracuse, was described as "one of the outstanding chinas in use in Midwest dining rooms."[120]

THE RESTAURANT BUSINESS

Running all of these restaurants required a significant investment in the food service industry. George Whinery oversaw a miniature kingdom that included cooks, waitresses, dishwashers, laundresses (to wash and iron the cloth napkins and tablecloths), a commissary and assorted support personnel. In 1949, preparing all of the food for both the Tea Room and the Garden Buffet fell to a relatively small kitchen staff: a head cook and second cook and three specialists for broiling, frying and vegetables (all men at this point). They were supported by an all-female pantry staff that assembled salads, handled coffee and fountain service, dished up desserts and polished silver. Bussing the tables and washing and rinsing the china, crystal and silver required a crew of twelve men and women.

Of the thirty-two waitresses who served in the Tea Room in 1949, nine were twenty-year veterans of the store and eleven were students working evenings. In the Garden Buffet, seven women served at the counter, two were at the fountain and nineteen "floor girls" waited tables.[121]

Although there was only one Tea Room, some branch stores included restaurants, too—the Meadowlark opened at the Merle Hay store in 1959; in 1963, the Charl-Mont opened in the downtown Kilpatrick's in Omaha; and both the Southridge Mall and Sioux Falls, South Dakota stores introduced a Peacock Room in 1975. These were all smaller than the restaurants at the downtown store but offered a convenient service for hungry shoppers. The Charl-Mont included a room intended for store meetings and private parties, but it was quickly claimed by men working downtown. The *Younker Reporter* quoted one of the customers as saying, "This is exactly what Omaha has needed, a place where men can come and enjoy a quiet, delicious meal." In 1980, the Merle Hay store introduced an alternative to fast food with 22 Carats, a sleek, contemporary restaurant offering an all-natural, health-conscious menu. The restaurant operated under the direction of Michael Lavalle, now one of the city's best-known culinary entrepreneurs and the Embassy Club culinary director.[122]

THE BEST BAKERY

The cinnamon rolls (with secret ingredient burnt caramel) were perhaps the most famous bakery item, but Younkers' Bake Shop also made many more items from scratch daily. In 1948, a new modern bakery opened on the fifth floor, separate from the Tea Room operations. In addition to stocking the retail counter on the first floor of the east building, the Bake Shop made "all the rolls, pies, cakes, biscuits, doughnuts, cookies, ice cream and special orders for the Tea room dining room, Garden Buffet, [and] Cremona Room." The 1949 *Younker Reporter* noted that "a day's volume is approximately 4,000 rolls of various kinds, 30 sheet cakes, 8 to 10 dozen pies, 30 dozen doughnuts, 50 dozen cookies, 3 to 4 gallons of pudding, and 10 or 12 sponge cakes." In addition, the bakery turned out angel food cakes, eclairs, patty shells and all sorts of special orders, as well as Younkers' own vanilla ice cream and one special flavor daily. The store could be justly proud of its bakers—they competed at the annual Iowa State Bakers' Association Convention and in 1975 won four first-place awards for wedding cakes, decorated cakes, breads and pastries, as well as an award for a wedding cake as the best overall creation.[123]

In late 1973 and early 1974, the entire fifth floor west got a facelift that enlarged and remodeled the Tea Room and eliminated the Rose Room. Part of the Rose Room space became a new bakery, and the rest was turned into the Sweet Shoppe, "a gourmet's glee and dieter's downfall," as described by the *Younker Reporter*. Decorated in a colonial style, the little shop served pastries, ice cream, finger sandwiches and freshly ground coffee between 11:00 a.m. and 3:30 p.m.[124]

Food service in one form or another continued to play a role at Younkers even after many other services and conveniences disappeared. The beloved Tea Room remained in operation until just before the downtown store closed in August 2005.

Chapter 8

FURNISHING THE IOWA HOME

In 1899, Younkers had begun selling household goods (lamps, pictures, china, glassware and "a thousand articles used every day in the home") and a very limited selection of furniture (bedsteads, sofas and specialty items). With the 1924 acquisition of the Wilkins Building, the store greatly expanded its furniture department and added an impressive array of decorating services. The new department was launched in August 1924 with "a sale that has been in the making for months," offering "hundreds of pieces of furniture on the large, spacious floor, with a warehouse abundance back of them," according to the ad in the August 7 issue of the *Des Moines Register*. Furniture could be purchased on the store's club plan with extended payments, putting it within reach of eager customers. Ads listed no brand names and simply promised "sturdy, reliable, trustworthy furniture with the good old reliable Younker quality at prices that spell REAL ECONOMY."[125]

Like other department stores, Younkers displayed its furniture in model houses, apartments and room settings constructed inside the store. The sets were outfitted in styles described as "classic-modern," "Early American" and "traditional," and the bachelor apartment from 1936 was "in the new modern manner." Store decorators Fred Hartsook and Florence Weaver usually oversaw the design and decoration of these model spaces.

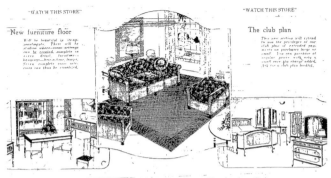

One of the important features of our Expansion Sale--
The opening within the next few days of our

New Furniture Section

WITHIN A FEW DAYS the new and complete Younker Furniture Section will make its bow to Des Moines and Iowa. It will be one of the most modern and picturesque departments of the kind to be found anywhere. Beautifully appointed--occupying more than 14,000 square feet of selling space and on an additional 20,000 feet of warehouse space--it will take its place in the front rank of the country's outstanding furniture sections.

Introductory Sale

TO OPEN IN A FEW DAYS WITH AN IMMENSE
AUGUST FURNITURE SALE

We plan to make this introductory August Furniture Sale a memorable event. You can await its opening with a quiet confidence that will be wonderfully rewarded. Our furniture head, a man of wide experience has been in the markets for over two months preparing--planning--coöperating with makers and promises values seldom if ever equalled in the ordinary run of furniture sales.

WATCH FOR THE OPENING DATE

Quality Furniture

NONE BUT THE PRODUCTS OF AMERICA'S
FINEST MAKERS WILL BE CARRIED.

No matter how much or how little furniture you may require--no matter whether your needs be for cottage or palace, you can be sure of finding an unexcelled choice of popular--medium priced--practical--dependable class of furniture, homemakers ever seek, as well as a notable display of the finest grades from America's most prominent and noteworthy cabinet makers.

WATCH FOR THE OPENING DATE

YOUNKER BROTHERS

The 1924 expansion into the Wilkins Building allowed Younkers to greatly enlarge its furniture department.

THE STORE FOR HOMES

During World War II, incomes in Des Moines reached all-time highs, but rationing meant there weren't enough things to spend it on.[126] Younkers executives could see that when the war ended, a huge demand would be unleashed, and the store would need additional space to offer more merchandise in greater varieties, particularly in home-related goods. In anticipation of that event, in August 1943 the company purchased the seven-story Oransky building on Eighth Street, diagonally across from and to the west of Younkers.

Home furnishings division merchandise manager William Friedman Sr. saw the building as an opportunity to greatly enhance Younkers' position in the home furnishings market. He persuaded company executives to devote the Oransky building entirely to furniture and home decorating merchandise. It would also house the decorating and home planning services.[127] The plan put Younkers in

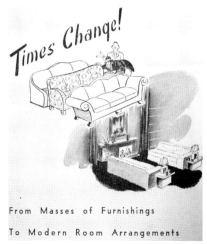

Left: A series of ads themed "Times Change!" built excitement for the opening of the new Store for Homes in 1946. *IVHC*.

Right: Younkers had shown furniture in room arrangements before, but the Store for Homes presented many more settings with a greater variety of styles. *IVHC*.

the forefront of a national trend in the years following the war, when a number of department stores expanded their furniture sections into complete stores. Younkers was among the first to do so.

Friedman and furniture buyer Robert Taggart made a dynamic team. Taggart had come to the store as a teen and started as a floor sweeper, working his way up to furniture buyer. Friedman had come to Younkers from Davidson's furniture store and built up the home furnishings business until it outgrew the space available in the main store. Together, they traveled the country, meeting with manufacturers; Taggart identified the lines and pieces people would want after the war, and Friedman negotiated the deals.[128]

By June 1946, the Oransky had been remodeled and renamed the Store for Homes. A subway under Eighth Street connected it to the main store. As opening day for the new store approached, Younkers embarked on a major advertising campaign with a series of full-page ads in papers across the state. Themed "Times Change," the ads proclaimed, "A new day dawns in home service for Iowans—Younkers' new STORE FOR HOMES comes into being—eight floors of furniture and home furnishings in a setting brighter than a new day! A store like none you've seen before."

Promotional materials emphasized the furniture displays as theater, with "every room in action." Friedman asserted that the Store for Homes was "the newest and most modern store of its kind in America." The trade magazines reiterated Younkers' explanation of what set this store apart: "No swimming seas of chairs. No train-like rows of sofas. All individual room arrangements as though in your own home, each room done with a decorator's flair, each one you visit more exquisite than the last." Because the fifth floor east furniture department had used room settings and model homes in the main store in the 1930s and 1940s, the concept wasn't actually new. But the sheer number of room settings—about fifty, each raised on its own platform and framed with walls—and the elaboration of individual color schemes tailored to each grouping took the selling technique beyond what customers were accustomed to. Another fifty-plus ensembles or mini-groupings were presented in front of pylons down the center of each furniture floor.[129]

The store was comprehensive, with everything related to decorating and outfitting a home. In addition to separate floors for dining rooms, living rooms and bedrooms, an entire floor presented window treatments, fabrics and slipcovers, and another floor showcased carpets, rugs and flooring. Appliances (arranged in those "old-fashioned" rows), kitchen cabinets and two model kitchens filled the basement, which also displayed record players, radios and records. The first floor greeted visitors with seasonal and fine furniture in room settings, and a large selection of lamps gleamed and glittered at the back. The main attraction on the seventh floor (besides the dining room sets) was the Ideal Farm Home, designed by *Successful Farming* magazine (published in Des Moines) using ideas submitted by more than one thousand farm families.[130]

When the store opened to the public for a sneak preview on Tuesday, June 11, thirty thousand visitors from all over the state came to see. The air conditioning wasn't working yet, so huge fans were placed throughout to help offset the summer heat. The next day, customers lined up outside two hours before the store opened, and the staff had to call on executives and trainees from the main store to help handle the crush of business. The July 1946 issue of *Furniture Index* reported that "total sales for both stores [the main store and Store for Homes] for the day were larger than in any event in the history of the store." Young couples were particularly interested in the appliances—vacuums, refrigerators, ranges, washing machines, dryers, heating units and the new "frozen food storage units." One of the great coups pulled off by Friedman and Taggart was the acquisition of mattresses. Because they were made out of steel and rubber, both of which were requisitioned for war production, mattresses were hard to come by. The Younkers duo managed to secure three or four boxcars full, and they sold out in two days.[131]

The Store for Homes offered customers well-known brands, a range of price points and modern style. *IVHC.*

Mrs. Ralph Moorehead, writing for *Retailing Home Furnishings*, commended the store for gearing its displays and merchandise choices to its home audience, Iowa. "Perhaps there have been displays more lavish shown in other cities," she wrote, "but the word 'practical' has been the watchword in buying merchandise, arranging displays and planning for the convenience of actual selling."[132]

If the store targeted a middle-class, largely rural consumer, it nevertheless appealed to well-heeled shoppers, too. Furniture brands included Lane, Stickley, Grand Rapids Chair Company, Kindel, Baker and Drexel. The fourth-floor Baker Gallery showcased high-end, eighteenth century–style reproduction furniture. The Studio Gift Shop

Room arrangements showed "furniture in action" to help customers picture it in their own homes. *IVHC.*

carried top-of-the-line brands such as Orrefors glass, International silver and Tiffany glassware, as well as internationally sourced art and antiques. The separate Marghab Linen Shop offered the exclusive line of museum-quality, hand-embroidered linens designed by Vera Way Marghab, a native Iowan.[133]

Although Early American and eighteenth-century English styles were consistently popular, Younkers introduced Iowans to contemporary furniture, too. In January 1948, it proudly presented the new Mengel Module furniture designed by Morris Sanders, the architect and designer who organized the first industrial art show at the Metropolitan Museum of Art. Hailed as the "newest thing since Chippendale," the sleek, upscale, modular units could be purchased separately and "assembled into hundreds of personalized pieces and reassembled at will."[134]

Responsibility for choosing all of the merchandise for the Store for Homes remained with Robert Taggart for many years. "For the better part of its existence, to most of the trade and to most of the customers, Mr. Taggart *was* the Store for Homes," recalled his son, Peter. "One of my favorite stories was when he would go to market, word would spread that he had picked up his badge, and old friends from showrooms would fan out to find him, to remind him not to forget to come and see them—and their line." Taggart's reputation for fair dealing and the relationships he cultivated with industry leaders helped build Younkers into "one of the largest furniture retailers in the nation" and "one of the most sought-after by manufacturers."[135]

DECORATING AND HOME DESIGN

As soon as Younkers expanded its furniture business in 1924, it began offering decorating services to businesses and individual home owners. Fred Hartsook and Florence Weaver, the store's professional decorators, handled theaters, lodges, hotels, churches, offices, public buildings and residences all over Iowa, as well as in neighboring states. Work ranged from choosing and installing new flooring, as for St. Paul's Episcopal Church and St. Ambrose Cathedral, to complete turnkey jobs, with the decorators making all of the decisions and overseeing installation of everything from paint, wallpaper and floor coverings to lighting, furnishings, fixtures and accessories. The department had its own picture framer, upholsterers, furniture refinishers and drapery workroom, so it could handle every aspect in-house. In 1940, the store participated in furnishing the largest apartment complex built in Des Moines up to that time: the Windsor Terrace apartments on Grand Avenue, completed in the fall of 1940. Younkers decorated four model apartments and, in a tidy piece of contract work, equipped each of the 136 units with a Frigidaire refrigerator and gas range.[136]

The store's decorating services were free if you purchased the goods from Younkers. In 1940, the store introduced an additional service, free assistance from the new home counselor, Miss Doris Young, who could "help you be your own decorator and keep within the budget." She offered help with color schemes, furniture selection and general decorating advice "to make rooms really livable…above all, keeping in the range of smaller incomes."[137]

Both the home counselor and the decorating services continued and expanded with the opening of the Store for Homes. In fact, the decorating services were described as "unique in Iowa" by the *Chicago Market News*. Eight interior decorators and additional consultants helped customers choose wallcoverings, paint colors, flooring, furniture and fabrics and oversaw the creation of custom window treatments, slipcovers and upholstery in the store's own workrooms. (A year after the Store for Homes opened, the decorating department split into two divisions, one for residential work and a second for institutional contract services to hotels, hospitals, colleges and restaurants.) Whatever a customer purchased from the Store for Homes, whether in person, by mail or by phone, could be delivered by Younkers' fleet of trucks, which went out to every county every ten days.[138]

Along with the decorating workrooms, the store maintained its own service department for the appliances, washing machines, radios and TVs it sold. By 1955, the workrooms and service department were churning out so much business that Friedman could state that "service and labor charges in the various workrooms amount to as much in a year as the annual volume of many smaller furniture stores. The Store for Homes is the only store in Des Moines conducting all these home services by the store's own personnel."[139]

THE AMERICAN DREAM

With experts predicting that seven out of ten families would be building new or remodeling their old residences as soon as materials became available after the war, home design seemed a fertile new field for the company. In preparation for the postwar building boom, Younkers opened a home planning center in the fifth floor east furniture department in early 1946, before the Store for Homes opened. As Mary Rodine, the home planning director, pointed out, selling house plans brought customers into the store at the beginning of the process, offering opportunities for selling paint, wallpapers and flooring as part of the planning.[140]

Younkers was one of forty-four department stores nationwide that teamed up with *Better Homes and Gardens* magazine to sell the publication's Five-Star Home Plans and the associated blueprints and building materials lists. The new home planning center also sold books on remodeling and maintained a reference library on home building and remodeling that customers were welcome to consult.

In addition to selling house plans, Younkers was in the vanguard of experimental efforts to solve the housing crisis. After World War II, most home builders still constructed homes one at a time—a practice that Congress blamed for the mismatch between demand and supply for housing in the late 1940s. The solution, it seemed, was to convert the housing industry to factory production methods.

Architects and magazines such as *Ladies' Home Journal* had been trying to persuade the American public to accept factory-produced housing since the mid-1940s.[141] In 1948, *Look* magazine took up the cause, creating a team to come up with a well-designed, tastefully furnished, factory-built home that would cost only $7,500. Walter Dorwin Teague, one of the most accomplished and influential architects and industrial designers in the country; Harry Levey, head of Adirondack Homes, a pioneer in prefabricated housing; and retailers willing to provide low-cost furnishings took up the challenge, producing the 1948 Look House. Model houses were built inside department stores, an armory and at Rockefeller Center in the Museum of Science and Industry. Des Moines was one of the first cities to participate in the project, and Younkers provided the interior decorating and furnishings.[142]

The 1948 Look House was available only through local Adirondack distributors, who were concentrated in the Northeast, Southeast and Midwest. Iowa had four distributors, one each in Charles City, Des Moines, Fort Dodge and Sioux Rapids. The house was designed to meet Federal Housing Administration guidelines and to qualify for FHA and GI loans.

That same year, Younkers Store for Homes participated in the debut of another experimental mass-production house: the first Lustron home in the Midwest. Built by H.B. Buckham & Company on Chamberlain Avenue in Des Moines, the porcelain-enameled steel house encompassed "five commodious rooms, plus utility room and bath" wrapped in a mint green shell with butter yellow trim. The "conservatively modern ranch-type" design aimed to please traditional tastes while nudging consumers toward modern design. Younkers furnished the interiors with modern pieces by Herman Miller, Grand Rapids Chair Company, Widdicomb and Heritage, noting that the home could be "tastefully furnished for about $2,000," although custom pieces shown in the Des Moines Lustron home cost more.[143]

Quite a few Lustron houses were built in Iowa, but the company was unable to produce and distribute the houses at a profit and declared bankruptcy in 1950.[144] The Chamberlain Avenue house and several others in Des Moines still stand, a little weary but icons nonetheless.

The housing crisis captured Hollywood's attention, too, inspiring the 1948 release of *Mr. Blandings Builds His Dream House* with Carey Grant and Myrna

Loy. The story was based on a popular Book of the Month Club title by Eric Hodgins. As part of a major promotional push for the movie, the studio built replicas of the nine-room colonial-style Dream House in sixty-five cities across the country, including Des Moines. Designed by architect Phil L. Boyle and constructed by builder R.H. Kenworthy, the house (which still stands at 4921 Woodland Avenue) was decorated and furnished by Younkers Home for Stores using American Provincial furniture shown in *House and Garden* magazine.[145]

Governor Robert D. Blue and Des Moines mayor Heck Ross attended the grand opening of the house on Sunday, June 6, four days before the movie debuted at the Roosevelt and Des Moines Theaters. The public could tour the house from June 6 through June 20 for an admission fee of fifteen cents, with proceeds going to the Des Moines Women's Club building fund. On the first day, 1,661 people visited the house.[146]

BRANCHING OUT

In 1971, Younkers decided to add a second Store for Homes at the Merle Hay Plaza, to compete with Pigeon's, the dominant furniture store in northwest Des Moines. The shopping center owners had decided to enclose the entire open-air shopping plaza, so it was a good time for Younkers to expand. The new store opened in October 1974 with "116 galleries of fine furnishings, plus appliances, draperies, carpets and lamps," all on one floor, reported the employee newsletter. "A special section of boutiques called 'Peacock Lane,' will specialize in pewter, bath accessories, linens, gifts, china and kitchen accessories."[147]

The downtown Store for Homes closed in 1985, but the Merle Hay Store for Homes continued operating until in 1991, when Younkers withdrew from the furniture and appliance business to focus on fashion.

FURNITURE WAREHOUSE

In 1973, a year before the Merle Hay Mall Store for Homes was completed, Younkers expanded its furniture business again with what it described as a new shopping concept for Iowa: the Younkers Furniture Showroom Warehouse.

The Furniture Showroom Warehouse opened in 1973. *MR.*

Operating independently of the Store for Homes, the Showroom Warehouse stocked first-quality, nationally recognized brands at low prices, at least 10 percent off regular retail prices on all merchandise. Customers could save an additional 8 percent by taking items home themselves, thereby avoiding delivery and setup charges. Another benefit: the Warehouse, located on First Street downtown, had plenty of free parking and generous hours, open until 9:00 p.m. on weekdays and open both Saturday and Sunday.[148]

Before embarking on the showroom warehouse approach, management had studied similar stores in major cities all over the country and was encouraged by their success. Aimed at recapturing business lost to the discounter Nebraska Furniture Market, the Warehouse presented furnishings in accessorized room settings, offering even more settings than the Store for Homes (150) and a wide variety of room types and furniture styles.

With the Store for Homes, Younkers had leaped ahead of the pack. Other retailers had seen the housing boom coming, but Younkers seized the opportunity to serve the new market and pursue its goal of growth at the same time. In the same way, it had been one of the first department stores after the war to open branch stores as a way of increasing presence, prestige and profits. In the decades that followed, Younkers became not only the largest store in Iowa but also the largest retail chain in the region, taking its policy of "Satisfaction Always" to Nebraska, Minnesota and beyond.

Chapter 9

A FULL-SERVICE STORE

Although Younkers had claimed to be simply a very large dry goods store in 1899, by the 1940s, it was offering a dizzying variety of goods supplemented by a host of related services, many of them unimaginable in today's department stores. In addition to buying shoes, you could visit a podiatrist for treatment of foot problems. Or you could take your old shoes to the shoe repair shop in the west basement, where Henry Pargas would work miracles to give them new life—clean or dye them, lengthen or widen them, make them shorter or narrower, replace or change heels, line, rebuild or refinish them.

During World War II, when nylon for stockings became impossible to acquire, the store opened a repair shop that could mend rayon, cotton, silk and even nylon stockings. If a garment didn't quite fit, the alterations or men's tailoring departments would adjust it free of charge, apparently as many times as necessary to get the fit right. (In 1982, re-alterations of men's clothing, sportswear and "related items" became subject to a charge—unless the original alteration was wrong and the item was returned within ninety days.)[149]

Need your watch repaired? Visit Younkers. Need an eye exam? Younkers' optician could check your eyes and fill your prescription for glasses. Stumped for gift ideas? Go to the Personal Service Bureau on the second floor west and talk to the gift counselor. She would not only make suggestions but would also do the shopping if you were pressed for time. At Christmas, Younkers brought in special assistant shoppers who helped customers find a single gift or complete their whole Christmas list. This, too, was free of charge. Planning a wedding? The Personal Service Bureau could advise on wedding etiquette and help with every aspect of planning. Brides could buy their invitations, dresses, flowers and wedding cake at Younkers and register for china, silver, crystal, linens and small appliances.[150]

The six staff florists in the flower shop made up fresh arrangements for every occasion—funerals, weddings, dinner parties and get-well wishes— and delivered them anywhere in town. Two of the staff graduated from Bright's School of Floristry and studied under Mrs. Tomoko Yamamoto, the city's authority on Japanese floral design.[151] The shop could also wire flowers anywhere.

Need a nice hostess gift? The Daylight Candy Kitchen made its famous chocolates and other confections daily in the factory on sixth floor east. One popular item was candy-by-the-yard, a three-foot-long package containing three pounds, ten ounces of Younker Brothers candy. Another favorite, the Younkerette, combined pecans, cream and bittersweet or milk chocolate. (In the 1950s, Younkers began carrying Kemps Candies, made by Lee Kemp, an African American candy maker whose factory stood at Seventh and Indianola Road.)[152]

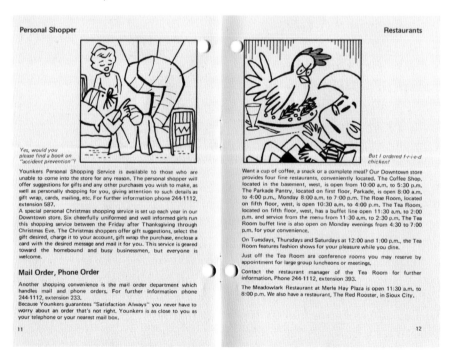

Customers who couldn't come to the store in person could enlist the services of a personal shopper or shop by mail. *CB.*

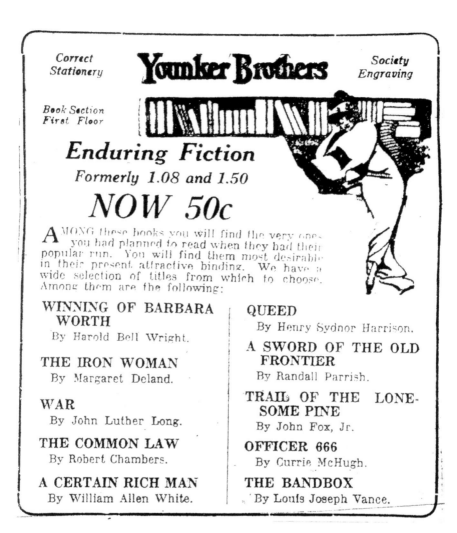

Younker Brothers

Correct Stationery

Society Engraving

Book Section First Floor

Enduring Fiction
Formerly 1.08 and 1.50

NOW 50c

AMONG these books you will find the very ones you had planned to read when they had their popular run. You will find them most desirable in their present attractive binding. We have a wide selection of titles from which to choose. Among them are the following:

WINNING OF BARBARA WORTH
By Harold Bell Wright.

THE IRON WOMAN
By Margaret Deland.

WAR
By John Luther Long.

THE COMMON LAW
By Robert Chambers.

A CERTAIN RICH MAN
By William Allen White.

QUEED
By Henry Sydnor Harrison.

A SWORD OF THE OLD FRONTIER
By Randall Parrish.

TRAIL OF THE LONESOME PINE
By John Fox, Jr.

OFFICER 666
By Currie McHugh.

THE BANDBOX
By Louis Joseph Vance.

Located on the first floor in 1914, the bookstore offered "correct stationery," as well as discounted reprints of popular fiction.

The increasing availability of affordable ready-to-wear didn't replace home sewing, and Younkers continued to sell fabrics by the yard, notions, dress patterns and sewing machines. If you bought your materials and patterns at Younkers, you could use its cutting tables and sewing machines for free and call on instructor Helen Thomas for help at no charge. The popular service averaged 200 to 250 appointments each month. After a 1941 remodeling that enlarged the workspace, 325 to 375 amateur seamstresses were signing up monthly.[153]

Younkers' Book Corner on the balcony, first floor east, stocked bestsellers and classics, as well as magazines. The rental library, housed in the same location, rented books for three cents per day, with a ten-cent minimum charge. In the basement west, the music department offered records and songbooks.

To allow for more relaxed shopping, the store provided a checking service for packages, bags and coats. There was normally a small fee for this service, but at Christmas it was free. Gift-wrapping, then as now, was available, but you could also ship packages, post a letter and cash a check at Younkers.

Services that might not fit the typical retail model—such as the optometrist, Salon François, Stark Travel Service and the Jean Sardou photo studio—were provided by outside organizations that leased space in the store. Salon François, with forty-five hair stylists, offered manicures, pedicures, facials and body treatments along with shampoo and styling in its shop on third floor west. There was even a "Make-Up Circle," where women could have their makeup refreshed free of charge, "an excellent 'pick-up' after a day of shopping…just before you go to dinner," suggested a customer service booklet.[154]

Stark Travel Service sold bus, train, air and steamship tickets; American Express travelers' checks; and money orders. The agency closed during World War II but reopened in 1945. By 1981, the renamed Younkers Travel Service could claim to be the oldest operating travel agency in Iowa. The year before, it had installed four airline computer terminals so it could print out airline tickets and itineraries in less than a minute. In 1981, it expanded its services to encompass chartered tours and cruises.[155]

The Jean Sardou photo studio, part of a chain based in New York, specialized in portraiture. In the 1940s, Younkers also offered a do-it-yourself photo service called the Photo-Reflex, an early version of the self-service photo booth. And to serve those pursuing the increasingly popular hobby of photography, the store sold cameras, film and photography supplies and offered same-day photo finishing services.

Although most of the services related in some way to the merchandise offered, others helped establish the store as a community center. On the first floor west, customers could leave messages for friends in a book on the entry table. If you needed to order a cab, the call was free. And of course, most visible and best known of the community center features were the Tea Room and restaurants, which offered meals, entertainment and places for groups to hold business meetings or social functions.

Gift Wrap

Will you gift wrap my hippopotamus?

Gift Wrap is available on 3½, west, at the accommodation desk. Here, you may receive deluxe gift wraps or courtesy gift wraps. Courtesy gift wraps are taken care of at this desk for those departments that do not have complete gift wrap facilities. This wrap consists of a white gift box with ribbon and bow. Courtesy paper is used only when the white gift box cannot be used.

You are entitled to a free deluxe gift wrap of your choice with a purchase of $25 or more. Simply take your sales slip with your purchase to 3½, west. There is a nominal fee for the deluxe gift wrap if the purchase is under $25.

At the accommodation desk you may also purchase bus passes, buy postage stamps or mail packages. (Refer to Postal Service.) Excessively large packages, such as the hippopotamus pictured above, are gift wrapped with a ribbon and bow.

For further information phone 244-1112, extension 468. Gift Wrap is available in all Younker stores.

Above: Stark Travel Service operated as a leased business at Younkers. *JC*.

Left: A booklet with a humorous take on the store's many services came from the 1971 graduates of the retail operations course. *CB*.

SHOPPING BY MAIL

For people who couldn't come to the downtown store, Younkers offered the Jane Wildner Personal Shopping Service. The fictitious shopper, inspired by a similar figure at Harris-Emery, was introduced in 1927 after the two stores merged. She added a personal touch to the thriving mail-order business that Younkers had been providing since at least 1899 and became a trusted friend to many mail-order customers over the ensuing decades. Customers could write or call to request merchandise, usually ordering items from the "Younkers Out-of-Town Shoppers Page," a weekly insert in the statewide edition of the *Des Moines Sunday Register*. "When you shop by mail or phone, you have the advantage of vast selections," noted a 1940s customer service pamphlet. "Seven floors of fine quality merchandise…apparel and home furnishings. Younkers prepays the postage in Iowa, so it costs no more to shop this easy way."[156]

Mail order, the foundation of business for retailers such as Sears Roebuck and Montgomery Ward, served Younkers well in terms of gaining national and even international recognition for the brand. The reliability of its service, no matter the distance, took on legendary proportions. The corsetry department had a regular customer in Nanking, China, whose size and preferred style were on record in the Younkers corsetry department. In 1950, thanks to the recommendation of a former Des Moines resident,

"Jane Wildner" gave the mail-order business a personal touch. In the 1940s, up to fifty people staffed the department. *MR.*

the department acquired Mrs. Hirohito, empress of Japan, as a customer. "Mrs. Hito ordered a nylon garment (the size cannot be revealed)," wrote Mabel Kutch in the *Younker Reporter*, "but we understood a slim neat figure was indicated. When the package arrived, it had to be thoroughly examined by the children's tutor before Mrs. Hito could open it." (Kutch's delight in having the empress as a customer may seem surprising given the anti-Japanese fervor of the war years. It indicates how effectively General Douglas MacArthur had suppressed evidence of the emperor's role in the war, for the sake of stability in Japan.)[157]

From the time Herman Younker opened the store in 1874, Younkers offered free delivery of purchases. The method changed—evolving from messenger boys to horse-drawn wagons to Younker trucks to an outsourced service, Retail Merchants Delivery—but the service was taken for granted by both customers and sales associates. In 1953, Younkers delivered nearly 1.2 million packages: more than half were within the city limits, nearly 300,000 were purchased at the store and delivered out of town and more than 363,000 were mail orders. By 1954, however, the convenience was becoming more expensive—an in-city delivery cost thirty cents and an out-of-town one forty-two cents, compared to a "take-with paper sack" at about half

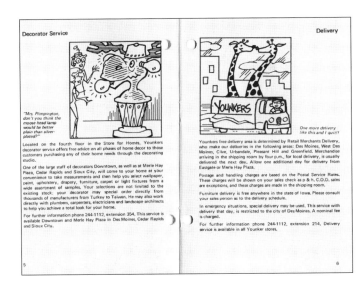

Decorator Service

"Mrs. Plimpington, don't you think the moose head lamp would be better plain than silver-plated?"

Located on the fourth floor in the Store for Homes, Younkers decorator service offers free advice on all phases of home decor to those customers purchasing any of their home needs through the decorating studio.

One of the large staff of decorators Downtown, as well as at Merle Hay Plaza, Cedar Rapids and Sioux City, will come to your home at your convenience to take measurements and then help you select wallpaper, paint, upholstery, drapery, furniture, carpet or light fixtures from a wide assortment of samples. Your selections are not limited to the existing stock; your decorator may special order directly from thousands of manufacturers from Turkey to Taiwan. He may also work directly with plumbers, carpenters, electricians and landscape architects to help you achieve a total look for your home.

For further information phone 244-1112, extension 354. This service is available Downtown and Merle Hay Plaza in Des Moines, Cedar Rapids and Sioux City.

5

Delivery

One more delivery like this and I quit!!

Younkers free delivery area is determined by Retail Merchants Delivery, who make our deliveries in the following areas: Des Moines, West Des Moines, Clive, Urbandale, Pleasant Hill and Greenfield. Merchandise arriving in the shipping room by four p.m., for local delivery, is usually delivered the next day. Allow one additional day for delivery from Eastgate or Merle Hay Plaza.

Postage and handling charges are based on the Postal Service Rates. These charges will be shown on your sales check as p & h. C.O.D. sales are exceptions, and these charges are made in the shipping room.

Furniture delivery is free anywhere in the state of Iowa. Please consult your sales person as to the delivery schedule.

In emergency situations, special delivery may be used. This service with delivery that day, is restricted to the city of Des Moines. A nominal fee is charged.

For further information phone 244-1112, extension 214. Delivery service is available in all Younker stores.

6

Until 1960, shipping was free for mail-order purchases. Delivery of items purchased in person was still free within a defined range as late as 1981. *CB.*

a cent and a box at six cents. Delivery errors because of sloppy writing or incorrect addresses also cost the company money. Rose Vernon, the delivery supervisor, urged sales associates to encourage customers to carry small purchases with them rather than automatically resorting to delivery.[158]

Free shipping for mail-order purchases ended in March 1960, when parcel post rates went up 17 percent, and the store began adding a shipping and handling charge to cover the cost. Free delivery still applied to items purchased in the store as late as 1981. Furniture delivery was also free anywhere in Iowa.[159]

As late as 1971, many of these services were still offered at the downtown store, as well as at selected branch stores. (At that time, there were twenty-one stores in all.) Some of the services that made Younkers the store for everything depended on the skills and training of just one or two specialists, and when that employee retired, the service was quietly retired as well. Rising minimum wages in the 1970s and 1980s also made some services too expensive to maintain, but as times changed, the store tried out new ways to provide old services. For You, a personalized fashion advice and shopping service for career women, debuted in April 1979. The twenty-five-dollar membership fee included a coupon book for a variety of services at the store. In 1988, the concept was reworked into a new department devoted to personal shopping, concentrating on service and individual attention. The specialized service was only available at Valley West, Merle Hay, Westroads East in Omaha, Crossroads and the downtown Des Moines store.[160]

SATISFACTION ALWAYS

In its heyday, the downtown store was an elegant emporium, an exciting place to visit, browse, dine and shop. The key to customer loyalty and satisfaction, however, depended on more than goods and services. From the president of the company on down, management impressed on employees the imperative of providing friendly, courteous service at all times, going the extra mile, being fair and decent. Exhortations to meet quotas on big sale days always ended with the reminder, "So keep this firmly in mind during the excitement of the big day…Wait on as many people as you can…but do not neglect, in any way, any Younker customer. Give smiling service always. Remember the Younker slogan—'SATISFACTION ALWAYS.'"[161] (This slogan began appearing under the Younkers name in newspaper ads as early as 1924.)

Company president Morey Sostrin told *Women's Wear Daily* in 1961, "Whatever we do should be the right thing to do in our ethics and our service. Temporary gain of dollars is secondary to the building and preservation of our most priceless asset—good will." The emphasis on service meant that Younkers carried a wide selection and followed "a liberal return policy… almost to the point of 'no questions asked,'" Sostrin explained. He admitted that the percentage of returns "probably runs about 2 percent more than that of other stores in our volume category…but this is a necessary consequence of our established policy: 'satisfaction always.'"[162]

One of Sostrin's favorite anecdotes about the lengths to which the store would go to make a customer happy featured an elderly woman who got a permanent in the beauty shop in August. "The following May she came to see me," recalled Sostrin, "saying she had never been happy with the permanent, although she had not said anything to any of our store people. By this time, her hair had grown considerably, of course, but I asked her if she would like the price of the wave refunded, or if she wanted another permanent. She took the permanent." Another example, cited in a *New York Times* article from 1966, sounds apocryphal: a woman wanted her money back for yarn she claimed was defective *and* she wanted to be reimbursed for the time she'd spent making a sweater she couldn't wear. Sostrin's orders: "Give the woman what she wants."[163]

The store's reputation for courtesy, thoughtfulness and attentive service often so impressed customers that they were prompted to write to express their thanks. Just one example: Mrs. Hazel Patterson of Cherokee, Iowa, praised "the courteous, helpful and friendly treatment that she had received from the girls in the basement men's furnishings section." In her experience,

YOUNKERS Good Morning

NEWS OF THE WEEK

VOL. I, NO. 7   DECEMBER 7, 1936

What to give? With thousands wondering what to buy for Aunt Agatha and Cousin Willie, it behooves all of us to be gift advisers. If we know our stocks well, suggested gifts that will be very satisfactory can be sold to those who are undecided. It is not suggested however, to insist that customers must buy from one just because they are undecided, but rather to be just as helpful as possible in making gift suggestions, regarding merchandise in your own section, especially. We must make our customers glad they came to Younkers for their Christmas shopping. We all can do that by courteous, helpful treatment to every one we contact.

Above: The weekly bulletin offered associates selling tips and reminders to offer courteous service at all times. *MR.*

Left: Surveys and opportunities for customer feedback helped Younkers fine-tune its employee training programs. *CB.*

Dayton's, Marshall Field's and Donaldson's didn't offer the same quality of treatment as Younkers. Associates at all of the branches were steeped in the same values and received similar compliments.[164]

And it wasn't just a matter of being pleasant and polite. When a shopper from Ames left her gloves on the counter at the downtown Des Moines store, "someone, following the tradition of Younkers for courtesy and thoughtfulness took the trouble to pack them as carefully as though they were a valuable purchase, and sent them to me," she wrote.[165]

Of course, no one is perfect all the time, and periodically, standards seem to have slipped. As World War II drew to a close, some longtime employees lamented that customer service wasn't what it used to be, and Morey Sostrin reiterated in several communications that one of the store's priorities was to return to the old standards of excellent, attentive service and "satisfaction always."

The late 1980s seem to have been another period of decline in customer service. Once things improved, it was so noticeable that customers wrote to the company about it. In 1991, a letter to then president Tom Gould read:

In a training tape, an associate shows how to fit a coat properly. *MR.*

Dear Mr. Gould: I just want you to know you have a customer back. I have had an account at Younkers since 1958. In recent years I have sort of drifted away from Younkers. It seemed like no stores were much interested in customer satisfaction. There were fewer clerks, and the attitude seemed to be "find it yourself and if I'm not too busy I'll take your money." I don't know who is responsible for the turn-around, but I've really been amazed by the changes in service at Younkers. Without exception, I've been treated so helpfully when I've shopped there in the past few months…I want to thank you for bringing back my old Younkers of the past and making it even better![166]

Another incident that year in Sioux Falls affirmed this return to the old Younkers-style service. Sales associate Bonita Christiansen helped a wheelchair-bound customer and her friends choose clothing during their first foray into the store, so in the fall, they called Bonita to tell her they were coming in again. When they arrived, she "had chosen several things I would deem suitable and I must say again her taste was very good," wrote the customer. "She was so helpful, even contacting other stores for a coat of a certain color which I had liked…Lucky Younkers…to have such a valued associate in your Sioux Falls store."[167]

Morey Sostrin would have been so proud.

Chapter 10

IOWA'S FASHION CAPITAL

In 1976, a junior at Hoover High School began a semester-long internship at Younkers, shadowing merchandise manager Joyce Mecham. The student, who was interested in a career in fashion retailing, was pleased to be placed at Younkers because it was "considered to be 'the fashion capital of Iowa—maybe even the Midwest,'" she said.[168] Although Chicagoans would surely argue with that assertion, it speaks to the reputation that Younkers enjoyed locally as a fashion leader.

In the 1970s and 1980s, customers had good reason to think of Younkers as the place for high style: the French Room carried Halston and Geoffrey Beene; their collections—along with those of Bill Blass, Yves St. Laurent and Diane von Furstenberg—appeared on the Tea Room stage, and by 1987, Gucci and Polo departments had been added to several of the branch stores.

FASHION SHOWS

One of Younkers' earliest innovations in selling women's fashions was the tea and style show in the Tea Room, introduced in March 1926. For fifty cents, customers could enjoy lunch and a fashion show with "living models" showing "what-is-what for spring.… The Fashion Tea was a decided innovation for Des Moines," the editor of the employee newsletter noted, "and one that evidently will call for a return engagement."[169]

The 1973 Christmas mail-order catalogue featured the stylish caftan, embraced by both hippies and haute couture designers. *CB.*

 HALSTON'S SHIRTDRESS. . .a top collector's item. It's Ultrasuede. . .the fabric which looks like suede, but behaves like the polyester it is. Newly zipped and typical of Halston's casual nonchalance in classic dressing. Chamois or forest green, 6 to 16, $240. French Room

Send Halston's Ultrasuede shirtdress at $240 in size____, chamois____, forest green____ (Please add 70¢ postage and handling, 3% tax in Iowa, 2.5% tax in Nebraska, local tax where applicable).

Charge ☐ Acct. No. _____ Check ☐ COD ☐

Name _____ Address _____

City _____ State _____ Zip _____

Call 244-1155 for 24-hour-a-day order service in Des Moines; or call your nearest Younkers store.

Left: Customers could order Halston's famous Ultrasuede shirt dress from the 1973 Christmas catalogue or find it in the French Room. *CB*.

Below: At the semiannual fashion clinics, employees modeled the new styles that associates would be seeing and selling. *DS*.

In 1985, the French Room presented spring and summer collections from Calvin Klein, Perry Ellis and others in the Tea Room. *MR.*

New York stores had introduced such style shows as early as 1903, imitating the Parisian fashion houses, and by 1914, department stores across the country were doing the same.[170] The Younkers lunchtime fashion show became a weekly staple, continuing through the Depression and World War II, when many other stores discontinued theirs, and into the succeeding decades. The models, who were Younker employees from various departments, often walked among the seated diners and talked about the style points of the items they wore. The informal presentation was relaxed yet entertaining and very popular. The store also organized more formal shows, with models on the runway.

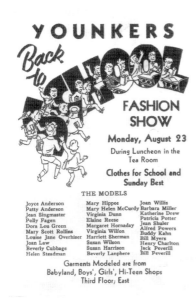

YOUNKERS

Back to SCHOOL

FASHION SHOW

Monday, August 23

During Luncheon in the
Tea Room

**Clothes for School and
Sunday Best**

THE MODELS

Joyce Anderson	Mary Hippee	Joan Willis
Patty Anderson	Mary Helen McCurdy	Barbara Miller
Jean Singmaster	Virginia Dunn	Katherine Drew
Polly Fagen	Elaine Reese	Patricia Potter
Dora Lou Green	Margaret Hornaday	Jean Shuler
Mary Scott Rollins	Virginia Wilfon	Alfred Powers
Louise Jane Overhiser	Harriett Sherman	Buddy Kahn
Joan Law	Susan Wilson	Bill Myers
Beverly Cubbage	Susan Harrison	Henry Charlton
Helen Steadman	Beverly Lanphere	Jack Peverill
		Bill Peverill

Garments Modeled are from
Babyland, Boys', Girls', Hi-Teen Shops
Third Floor; East

Back-to-School fashion shows tapped
local youngsters for modeling talent. *CB.*

In August, back-to-school fashion shows featured new outfits for toddlers to teens, and a separate show highlighted collegiate fashions. For the children's show, the store recruited child models from employee families and the community, and in 1937, Bill Peverill and his younger brother, Jack, were among the thirty children asked to participate. Peverill, now a well-known Des Moines businessman and raconteur, later wrote that he and his brother were to bow to the audience and then walk down the runway together, pausing for turns to give the audience a full view of the outfits. "When the time came for the first turn," he recalled, "I turned but my brother Jack was motionless. Then (with a glance to my mother and her luncheon party), I said to him, 'Jack, you are supposed to turn.' At the next turn juncture, I became more aggressive, giving Jack a nudge and with greater emphasis, 'JACK, you are supposed to TURN!!' Jack then hit me. Then I hit him back. A slugfest ensued. We became the show's greatest attraction. That is, to all but my mother."[171]

Child models aside, the Tea Room style shows helped establish Younkers as a fashion authority, and the store also put on shows for outside organizations and events, such as the Des Moines Women's Club and the annual Des Moines Auto Show at the Coliseum. After the war, when Younkers began planting branch stores around Iowa, the fashion coordinator and employee-models from the Des Moines store took the style shows on the road, with all the fanfare of a celebrity event. In 1947, the modeling team captured media attention by flying to Mason City on Mid-Continent Airlines to present a vacation-wear style show at the Hotel Hanford. The models were escorted from the airport to the hotel in new convertibles, and an audience of four hundred enjoyed a comprehensive review of travel clothes, play clothes, sportswear, lingerie and evening dresses.[172]

Beginning in the early 1950s, branch stores began organizing their own fashion events, drawing on the expertise and fashion-clinic lessons offered at the

A. "MODERN CERAMICS" . . . black rayon
faille suit with ceramic costume buttons. 12 to
20. 59.95

—Suit: Second Floor, East

B. "PORTRAIT OF A YOUNG LADY" . . .
David Crystal's striped chambray with white pique
top. Pink or blue, with white. 10 to 16. 22.95

C. "ABSTRACTION" . . . block print by David
Crystal, black with blue, purple or tan predomi-
nating. 10 to 18. 22.95

This 1948 fashion ad paired Younkers' fashion and the art at the new Des Moines Art
Center, "both significant in the trend of tomorrow." *IVHC.*

main store. Younker-Davidson's in Sioux City, which had its own buyers, was
particularly active in promoting fashion through style shows. Its efforts included
co-presenting an annual spring bridal show with *Mademoiselle* magazine and,
in 1960, organizing a panel of store experts to give a fashion presentation
inspired by the television show *What's My Line?* The panel entertained groups
such as the Quota Club, the Officers' Wives Club at the Sioux City Airbase
and the Faculty Wives Club of Sioux City Junior and Senior High Schools.[173]

Style shows, whether in the Tea Room or in branch stores, were usually accompanied by live music and commentary, but in 1978, the production ballooned into a musical extravaganza. A production titled *The Best of the West* highlighted the West Coast lines the store carried, with twenty models, disco music, singing and dancing in front of various California scenes. The show kicked off with a wine and cheese party in the Tea Room (admission: $2.50) and then went to Southridge and Merle Hay Malls in Des Moines and on to Dubuque and the Quad Cities.[174]

The following year, another, even more ambitious musical, *The You You're Looking For*, promoted junior and young men's fashions for fall. The program called for twenty-eight employees who could not only model but also sing and perform choreographed dance numbers. The thirty-five-minute show required thirty-five hours of rehearsal, two days of fittings and a half-day of dress rehearsals before the premiere on August 2 in the downtown Tea Room. Over the next five weekends, the cast traveled by bus to thirteen cities in four states. The models/singers/dancers were also the crew, loading and unloading the props, sound equipment and the more than 150 outfits and accessories at each stop. After each performance, the cast often joined sales associates on the selling floor to help promote the lines just presented.[175]

SOURCING STYLE

Before World War II, Younkers looked to the Amos Parrish Fashion Merchandising Clinics in New York for advice on fashion trends and which lines of apparel to stock. Parrish was one of several independent consultants versed in the emerging business of publicity, promotion and modern selling techniques. In the late 1920s, he began holding the Amos Parrish Clinics for merchandising and advertising managers, buyers and display managers. Once and often twice a year, participants from across the country gathered to hear his insights into trends and learn how to sell fashion effectively.[176]

How Younkers chose Parrish is unknown—there were at least two other well-known retailing consultants in New York City. Macy's, Gimbels and Federated counted on Tobé Collier Davis, whose daily broadcast on fashion trends "was the most sought-after service of its kind in the business." Younkers, however, relied on Amos Parrish from 1930 until the clinics stopped in 1956.[177]

In the 1940s, full-page ads featured fashion illustrations created by Younkers' own artists. *IVHC.*

Like department stores across the country, Younkers also looked to Paris for fashion guidance, but unlike other stores, it did not have a buying office in Paris. In 1933, however, the store sent its own buyer, a Miss Farrell, to Paris to scout for merchandise. Two years later, Eloise Veneman, the millinery buyer, took a six-week trip to Europe and brought back thirty-two hats from Paris to sell at the store. Creations by major designers—including Molyneux, Jean Patou, Alphonsine, Marthe, Lewis, Valmonde and Blanche Simonne—were obtained "through Miss Veneman's personal connections." She also had lunch with the famed Lily Daché, an enormously influential millinery designer who later mentored Halston and whom Veneman "found to be charming as well as a famous stylist."[178]

Along with these early forays into the European markets, Younkers looked to American designers for its style-forward fashions. And what better source of inspiration than Hollywood? Younkers was the first store in Des Moines, and possibly the Midwest, to introduce its customers to the controversial new trouser suits made famous (or infamous) by Marlene Dietrich. Hollywood actresses such as Greta Garbo and Katharine Hepburn had begun wearing men's-style trousers and flowing pajama pants in public by 1930, but when Marlene Dietrich appeared in a man's tuxedo at the premier of *The Sign of the Cross* in 1932, it caused an uproar. It also launched a "trouser craze" for women.[179]

Fashion buyer Howard Lyon brought the trouser suit to the Younkers Misses' Shop in 1933, and it was featured in the Des Moines Auto Show fashion revue and at a College Club dance at the Tea Room. The March 1933 employee newsletter noted that many women were trying them on. "The question is," wondered the editor, "will women accept trousers for evening and for street wear?"[180] (It seems the answer was probably not.)

The store's reputation for taste and style was affirmed in 1934 when Frances Perkins, the U.S. secretary of labor, came to Des Moines. Descending from the train, she told a companion that she needed a new hat, so the woman took her to Younkers, where she purchased a black velvet beret. "Wearing the new hat in the east a few days later she received recognition of it in many newspapers, including the *New York Times*," reported the *Des Moines Tribune*.[181]

After World War II, California became an increasingly important source for fashion, and Younkers sent more buyers to the West Coast as the decade progressed. In 1946, the downtown store staged its first California-focused store-wide, weeklong promotion, "From California to You," featuring clothing from leading California manufacturers and designers. Women's clothing and accessories were modeled in the Tea Room, and the men's department showcased men's wear and "typical western items" as well.[182]

As fashion became increasingly important to the store's core business, forecasting fashion trends required a full-time fashion director. *MR.*

As part of the California promotion, the store took out a full-page advertisement in the first issue of *The Californian*, a magazine published in Los Angeles by Henry Frankel's son-in-law. The ad was part of a new advertising strategy to gain national recognition and prestige for the store. Full-page ads featuring branded apparel at Younkers for women and college women appeared in *Vogue, Glamour, Harper's Bazaar, Mademoiselle* and *Junior Bazaar* in 1946. *Fashion Trades Weekly* took notice of the national ad campaign and commented on the "unusually large line of nationally advertised apparel" that the store carried in order to serve a clientele that took in the whole state. The campaign splashed Younkers' name across the country and also brought sales—customers could order by mail or by phone the items shown in the ads, and the store's growing mail-order service would wrap them up and ship them out.[183]

THE FRENCH ROOM

Recognizing the cachet of Paris fashion in the late 1920s, Younkers began using the term "the French Room" to designate spaces set aside for couture or luxury items as early as 1933. The hats Veneman brought back from Paris were destined for "the French Room." The Corset Shop gained its own such boutique in 1934, with private fitting rooms at the back of the department and a comfortable waiting room.[184]

Although it was never explicitly mentioned in employee communications, the French Room concept must have been abandoned during World War II. In his message to employees in February 1945, Morey Sostrin,

Younkers' new president, seemed to suggest it would be reinstated, noting, "We will add an exclusive Salon for presentation of distinctive apparel and accessories. This will really be a high grade specialty shop within our store. We will also have a shop for brides." An article in the *Fashion Trades Weekly* in 1946 noted that Helen "Polly" Pollock, the store's fashion coordinator, "has a plan for something super in a glamour department. There, not only would exclusive gowns be shown, but the very best in accessories as well. The Younker's customer could complete her ensemble in one department." The idea of a French Room—an upscale department serving a discriminating clientele—was common to department stores such as Marshall Field's, Bloomingdale's, Dayton's and Saks. In addition to conferring prestige, it "created a fashion umbrella, which helped sell similar things at lower price ranges" elsewhere in the store.[185]

On September 15, 1948, a new French Room opened formally on the fifth floor east of the downtown Younkers. The event included a style show in the Tea Room, titled "New Horizons in Fashions," for a paying audience of six hundred women. The two-dollar tickets benefited the Raymond Blank Memorial Hospital Guild, possibly the first instance of fashion at Younkers benefiting a charitable cause and setting a precedent for fundraisers in the

Reopened on fifth floor east in 1948, the French Room was remodeled in 1971. *CB.*

1960s and 1970s. The garments were modeled by Younker's own team, the Stylettes, and members of the hospital guild, with commentary by Connie Weber, the associate editor of *Vogue* magazine.

To design the boutique, Younkers hired Raymond Loewy Associates, which had created store designs for Saks Fifth Avenue, Lord & Taylor, Macy's and Bloomingdale's. The new French Room was clearly intended to enhance the store's prestige as a style leader, but with typical midwestern modesty, the company wanted to avoid any hint of elitism. The *Younker Reporter* emphasized that the shop was designed to feel welcoming and approachable as well as elegant, and it declared the new space "a triumph in combining the modern and traditional with such artistry that the décor is that of charm rather than exclusiveness."[186]

Mannequins by Christian Dior displayed American designer clothing, including Ted Stein, Fred A. Block, Eisenberg and Rothmoor, who were well-regarded Chicago designers. Nettie Rosenstein, however, was the most prestigious label represented. She emerged in the late 1920s as one of the most influential designers in American fashion, with her "Little Black Dress" and other designs that were widely copied. Her prestige was such that she could afford to be very choosy about which retailers received exclusive rights to carry her label. Younkers had scored a coup in becoming one of the ninety-two department stores and shops across the country granted that privilege in 1940.[187]

Younkers' French Room merchandise could hold its own in Paris. Florence Miller, one of the boutique's longtime sales associates, heard from one of her customers touring Europe in 1950, "We attended the spring fashion show of Christian Dior. I'm still happy with the clothes you sold me. They have done all right in Geneva, Monte Carlo, and now in Paris."[188]

In 1952, the new French Room buyer, Gladys Omen, attended two openings in Los Angeles, one at the much sought-after Adrian's and the other at Howard Greer's. Along with Edith Head, Adrian was one of the most famous costume designers in Hollywood in its golden age. As head costume designer for MGM, he created glamorous outfits for Greta Garbo, Joan Crawford, Jean Harlow, Lana Turner and Katharine Hepburn among others and designed Dorothy's ruby slippers in *The Wizard of Oz*.

Omen told the *Younker Reporter*, "No one but Mr. Adrian asks of his carefully selected accounts that they pack one evening gown and tux to appear at an 8:30 showing." Entering his showroom, "decorated in the softest pale green from carpet to ceiling," and viewing his originals gave her goosebumps. She ordered for the store some coats, suits, a basic dress and a theater gown called the "Golden Moon."[189] Unfortunately for Younkers, the 1952 collection was Adrian's last; he retired that year after suffering a heart attack and died a year later.

Omen's other trophies included selections from the collection of Howard Greer, another Hollywood costume and fashion designer; bridal gowns from William Cahill of Beverly Hills; and luscious suede coats from Voris, who had received the Neiman Marcus Fashion Award in 1942.

In 1953, the French Room added a new section for "exclusive fashions in separates, accessories, and jewelry. Exciting high fashion merchandise created by well-known designers will be featured in this new shop," according to the employee newsletter. Little mink collars and stoles featured prominently as accessories for suits, dresses and sweaters. Jewelry and embroidered sweaters from Rex Inc. of California, handmade cashmere sweaters trimmed with pearls or blue fox fur and a Voris-designed twenty-five-carat-gold kid jacket for evening wear were among the treasures available.[190]

The French Room concept was also extended that year to the millinery department on the second floor west, with a new boutique described as "one of the few millinery boutiques in the country. The idea in creating a

The French Room Boutique showcased exclusive designer labels in an elegant setting. *CB.*

'little shop' is to offer the customer unusual items that are related in anyway to anything pertaining to head gear or head coverings—however frivolous and unnecessary." It was clearly a year that celebrated the frivolous for head gear: tie-on jeweled veils, sequin-sprinkled netting "to drape over your head and shoulders when you 'go formal'" and gray fox leis were among the new items on offer. Some were created exclusively for Younkers, such as hand-dipped and tinted cocktail veils. The casually cluttered display invited customers to browse and make their own selections, although sales associates were always at the ready to provide the personalized service that was a Younkers specialty.[191]

In 1970–71, a major remodeling of the fifth floor east moved the French Room to a position behind its original spot, which was entirely rebuilt for a better-dress shop. When Younkers opened large branch stores in high-end suburbs such as Davenport and Omaha, it introduced French Rooms there as well.[192]

CUSTOM CLOTHING

Since the late 1880s, Younkers not only sold fur coats and wraps but also maintained a workroom staffed by furriers and finishers. They altered new coats to fit and reworked customers' old furs, lengthening, shortening or refashioning coats into capes as style demanded. The department occupied space on two floors, with a main reception room on the sixth floor east and the workroom on the balcony. The furriers could also custom-make coats from hides brought in by trappers and had two storage vaults where "nearly 10,000 fur coats are stored during the summer."[193]

Perhaps one of the store's best-kept secrets was its custom dressmaking service, which operated under the leadership of Mrs. Sadie E. Byrd from 1927 until 1953. Mrs. Byrd had learned dress design in St. Louis and came to Des Moines in 1918 as a dressmaker for the Dallas Company. She joined Harris-Emery in 1922 and transferred to Younkers with the merger in 1927. At that time, she oversaw a sewing and fitting department of eighteen; at her retirement, a sewing and alterations staff of forty-three occupied modern workrooms in the annex.

As a dressmaker of the old school, she seldom used patterns, preferring to devise her own. After planning and fitting the garment to suit the client, she turned the sewing over to her assistants. At her retirement, Mrs. Byrd told the *Younker Reporter* that perhaps "25 of her leading customers left the choice of fabric and design up to her, simply stating, 'I want five new dresses. Will you please pick out whatever you think I should have and call me when you're ready to give me a fitting?'" She never had any complaints.

Some of her favorite work involved custom dresses for large weddings. "Almost all the brides I outfitted in this last season were daughters of brides of a generation ago I had served in the same way," she said. She recalled an evening dress for a Des Moines bride "just arrived from Europe. Her dress caused much comment at the party, she said, as everyone thought it had been brought from Paris." Mrs. Byrd's retirement ended the custom-sewing service for Younkers, and thereafter the department offered only alterations.[194]

The Youth Market

Before World War I, a youth market didn't exist as far as retailers were concerned. Clothing for babies and children was generally made at home, and there was no concept of the teenager. In this period, Younkers was already aware, however, of an emerging market for clothes designed especially for girls at the in-between stage—too old to be considered children but still developing physically. An ad in the February 11, 1910 *Evening Tribune* announced with flowery enthusiasm a collection of dresses for girls: "Never before have the styles for girls been so well adapted to their youthful figures—never before has the genius of master designers conjured effects so pleasing to the eye nor more becoming to their age."

In the mid-1920s, Younkers began reaching out to the younger consumer with an illustrated monthly, the *Juvenile Magazine*. Its poems, cartoons and short stories, packaged between promotions for boys' and girls' clothing and toys, addressed a range of ages.

The 1924 enlargement of Younkers to incorporate the Wilkins Building allowed the store to introduce entirely new departments, including a misses' and girls' department on the third floor. There still was no separate college shop, but the store acknowledged college girls as a distinct category. August 1924 newspaper ads promoted clothes for "every activity and every requirement of the collegienne wardrobe—campus togs, class room frocks, dinner and party costumes." Ten years later, Younkers recognized the distinctive needs of girls in the "hi-teen" bracket, ages ten to fourteen,

Left: Younkers recognized the distinctive needs of the youth market in the 1910s and began targeting it with a magazine for children in 1925. *CB.*

Right: Illustrations and stories personalized fashion for kids. *CB.*

carving out a new department that offered "the longer fitted styles for high school girls," as well as an intermediate "half size…to make plump girls look like wafers." Younkers may have been slightly ahead of department stores back east in introducing this category; Strawbridge & Clothier didn't distinguish between its "junior miss" and girls' departments until 1937.[195]

With the 1939 modernization program, the youth market finally emerged as a clearly separate category. The third floor east was entirely re-conceptualized as the "Young America Floor," with separate shops for College, Hi-Teen, Girls, Boys, Prep and Children, as well as Babyland.

To tap into the buying power and influence of college women, department stores established college boards. Active during the summer months, the Younkers board consisted of eight to ten young women attending both Iowa and out-of-state colleges. The board's job was to advise freshman girls on items they would need for school and where to find them in the store. Board members also collaborated on scripts for back-to-school fashion shows and radio broadcasts and presented their own campus fashion show in the Tea Room.

In the early 1940s, Younkers extended the board concept to high school girls and, in 1965, introduced an advisory board to bring boys into the Younkers fold. Like the college boards, the teen and advisory boards represented the store in their schools, advised their peers on fashion and

Youth Boards Begin 1973-74 Season in Des Moines Stores

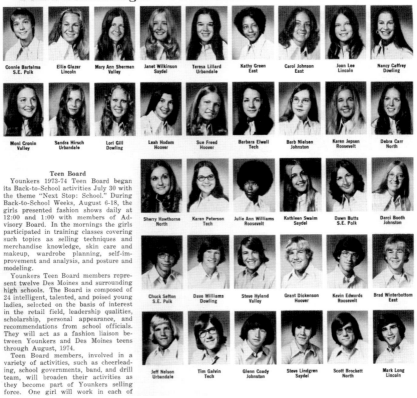

Teen Board

Younkers 1973-74 Teen Board began its Back-to-School activities July 30 with the theme "Next Stop: School." During Back-to-School Weeks, August 6-18, the girls presented fashion shows daily at 12:00 and 1:00 with members of Advisory Board. In the mornings the girls participated in training classes covering such topics as selling techniques and merchandise knowledge, skin care and makeup, wardrobe planning, self-improvement and analysis, and posture and modeling.

Younkers Teen Board members represent twelve Des Moines and surrounding high schools. The Board is composed of 24 intelligent, talented, and poised young ladies, selected on the basis of interest in the retail field, leadership qualities, scholarship, personal appearance, and recommendations from school officials. They will act as a fashion liaison between Younkers and Des Moines teens through August, 1974.

Teen Board members, involved in a variety of activities, such as cheerleading, school governments, band, and drill team, will broaden their activities as they become part of Younkers selling force. One girl will work in each of

Teen Boards included representatives from all area schools. *CB.*

planned and participated in fashion shows. The teens also worked at the store part time, selling apparel and earning points that might qualify them for cash prizes at the end of the year. The boards helped the store stay in touch with the increasingly important and powerful youth market and helped increase sales in those departments. For the young people involved, it was a tremendous opportunity to gain work experience, indulge an interest in fashion and style and develop poise and professionalism in dealing with people. (Members were also eligible to represent Younkers on national boards and councils such as the Bobbie Brooks National Fashion Council and the *Seventeen* Fashion Council. Serving at the national level not only gave Iowa teens the chance to compete for scholarships but also brought national attention to Younkers itself.)[196]

A 1985 fashion illustration from the *Younkers Reporter*. MR.

BRINGING BACK THE IMPORTS

In 1962, some thirty years after the first Younkers buyers traveled to Paris for the store, the company ventured back into buying directly from overseas vendors. Sportswear buyer Helen Mossholder was the first emissary to the European markets. She was accompanied by a representative of the store's new consultant, the Mutual Buying Syndicate in New York. After this successful foray, the store sent additional buyers to Asia and Europe, moving rapidly beyond women's fashion to include men's furnishings, toys, housewares, stationery and leather goods. The men's buyer didn't bother with readymade goods, instead working with manufacturers to develop custom lines.[197] By the late 1960s, Younkers really did bring the world to Iowa, with a wide array of goods imported directly from the source.

Chapter 11

SOMETHING IS ALWAYS HAPPENING AT YOUNKERS

In the mid-1990s, Des Moines businessman Bill Peverill noted that early on Younkers learned "the key to retailing success: Make your store a fun place to visit."[198] The more often people could be enticed to the store, the more likely they were to buy something—and enjoy themselves in the bargain.

WINDOW SHOPPING

Before shoppers even entered the store, they had a good reason to stop at Younkers. The fourteen- by twenty-one-foot display windows that lined three sides of the downtown building were like shallow stage sets, with sills so close to the ground you could almost step right in.

The Christmas windows were as famous in Des Moines as those of Bloomingdale's and Lord & Taylor's were in New York City, filled with animated figures created especially for Younkers or purchased from Marshall Field's.[199] In 1978, Jean Keiter of Stark Travel recalled Younker's "magic window," an annual destination when she was growing up in Des Moines. "Every Christmas we would go see the Younkers' big window display with Santa on his throne. No matter how many other Santas we would go see around town, my sister and I wouldn't consider giving our orders to anyone but Younkers' Santa in the window."[200] The rest of the year, most of the windows showcased merchandise, but a variety of educational

Younkers' Christmas windows were a highlight of the season. *SHSI*.

and civic-minded displays were presented as well. These "public service announcements" ranged from the city's new parking regulations to safe driving, interfaith dialogue, gun registration, Shriners, Rotary Club and the history of business.

For thirty-five years, Maurice Swander was in charge of trimming these windows, and as branches were established, he and his staff dressed their windows as well. In 1947, Swander received the Socrates Award from *Modern Display*, a monthly trade publication for retail store display directors. The award was considered a "highly coveted honor" in the advertising world. In 1954, Swander's work again won recognition with two bronze medals in an international display contest sponsored by a regional trade magazine.[201]

CELEBRITIES SELL

Bringing in celebrities increased store traffic, and over the years, Younkers created events large and small around visiting luminaries. Tennessee Ernie Ford and Spike Jones attracted fans to the music department. Eva Gabor and Diane von Furstenberg drew crowds to the cosmetics and fashion departments. Miss Universe visited in 1955, 1956 and 1957 as a representative of the Catalina brand of swimwear to talk about new swimwear styles. Miss America made appearances to promote "made in America" merchandise. Even minor celebrities, such as Lawrence Cross, aka Merrio the Clown, could add extra excitement to the already irresistible thrill of Toyland at Christmas.

In 1975, the Southridge Mall branch store began partnering with Kodel, a polyester fiber manufacturer, to present an annual mixed-doubles tennis tournament that brought players from all over the state. International tennis stars such as John Newcombe made guest appearances at the Des Moines stores, and well-known players, including Frank Parker and Bill Talbert, came out of retirement to play exhibition games and lead

Page 10 — THE YOUNKER REPORTER

Toyland Across Eighth Street on First Floor of "Store for Homes"

Top picture: The Christmas edition of Younkers Toyland is again this year on the first floor of the new "Store for Homes" across Eighth street. View is taken from the front door look- | ing west. Lower picture: Center of Toyland from the north wall looking south. Lawrence Cross, as Merrio the Clown, is shown in the center of the picture.

Even Toyland benefitted from visits by celebrities (in addition to Santa). Merrio the Clown welcomed shoppers in 1945. *CB.*

107

tennis clinics. As the *Younker Reporter* recognized, "When these unusual events happen they create an atmosphere of excitement in the store. This air of 'something always happening at Younkers' entertains and pleases our customers."[202]

Celebrities were just one means of making the store a destination. Younkers followed the lead of department stores across the country and became an entertainment emporium, local art gallery, educational center and lending library as well.

MUSIC, DANCING AND MORE

Thanks to the Tea Room, Younkers was the place to go for live music, dancing and fun. In the 1930s, every Friday night was College Club Night, with Doc Lawson and his orchestra playing from 9:15 p.m. to midnight. Sometimes, Otis Wyatt, one of the restaurant busboys by day, entertained with song and dance routines at night.[203]

Theater Nights, introduced in the late 1930s, proved to be a long-lasting, popular tradition that attracted national attention. An article in the *Woman's Home Companion* that was picked up by *Reader's Digest* in February 1937 described the event as a solution for young people looking for something fun and affordable to do. Theater Nights, however, served a much broader clientele than the youth. The Tea Room opened at 6:00 p.m. (after the store had closed) every night except Sundays and holidays. For one dollar per person, customers could enjoy a four-course dinner, dance to the music of a nine-piece orchestra and then receive a ticket to one of three movie theaters downtown. "By nine," wrote author Anna Steese Richardson, "the dinner crowd has scattered to the movies, more rugs are rolled back to make larger dancing spaces, and young people pour in for the 'late dance' from 9:30 until 12. This costs one dollar a couple. Soft drinks and sandwiches may be purchased." The magazine pointed out that this service to the community meant that the store had to keep all of the doors open, special elevators operating (with the attending operator) and guards on each floor, so the likelihood of Theater Nights being profitable was exceedingly slim. "But this unusual service has made of Younkers' in Des Moines a social institution and a rendezvous for women's groups," not to mention couples looking for economical entertainment.[204]

The Tea Room also hosted special events designed to entertain and educate. In 1940, a wartime focus on countries under siege in Europe may have inspired the presentation of a "Czecho-Slovakian Evening" featuring costumed folk dancers, a Czech dinner, a "choir in colorful costume singing native folk songs" and a movie about Czechoslovakia, all for $1.50. The following year, South America took center stage, with dinner "as you would order it in Brazil (or Iowa as you prefer)," music by Barney Barnard and his orchestra, a rumba demonstration and both color and black-and-white travelogues on "Western South America, Gay Panama, Peru, Bolivia and Chile," as well as Cuba, the West Indies, the Guianas and Brazil—all for $1.00 per person (almost $17.00 in 2015 dollars). For more modest cultural entertainment, book lovers could attend a book review with Mrs. Edith Dunham Webber in the Tea Room—$0.50 on Wednesday evening or $0.50 with tea on Friday afternoon.[205]

ART AND CULTURE

While the Tea Room symbolized all that was gracious and elegant about Younkers, throughout the store there were features that helped turn shopping into something more than a hasty transaction. A piano player performed outside the Cremona Room in the basement, and white-gloved elevator operators delivered shoppers to their destinations (in what were described as some of the slowest elevators in town). Uniformed operators were still running three of the five manually operated elevators for sales associates to use in 1985. (The other eight elevators had been replaced with self-serve "automatics" in 1967.)[206]

The foyer outside the Tea Room became a gallery for showcasing original art. Every few weeks, a new exhibit appeared on the walls, featuring the work of Iowa artists, art teachers and students; Younkers' own advertising artists; and borrowed or traveling collections such as paintings by an Alaskan artist and Eastman photos described as "nationally famous." Sometimes the works were for sale; at least once, Younkers made the foyer available to the Junior League to sell art prints as a fundraiser. The company also sponsored the Iowa division of an annual art contest put on by *Scholastic* magazine.

Uniformed elevator operators added elegance and grace to the shopping experience and were important to making Younkers "the friendly store." *MR.*

MOVIE TIE-INS

Movie tie-ins offered an ideal opportunity for entertainment that doubled as promotion. On the January 1940 evening that *Gone with the Wind* opened in Des Moines, some of Younkers' younger employees modeled costumes from the film for a special Tea Room event. In 1945, the movie *State Fair* premiered in Des Moines on August 29, and the store joined the citywide celebration, decorating four of its street-level windows with special movie-related displays. On the afternoon of the big day, about one thousand eager fans packed the Tea Room for a fashion show featuring actress Carole Landis and the five finalists for the Miss State Fair title. Younkers also entered a float in the evening parade that preceded the premiere.[207]

Movies with a lavish nostalgic fashion element also inspired store events. In April 1974, '20s style took center stage when Francis Ford Coppola's production of *The Great Gatsby*, starring Robert Redford and Mia Farrow, and *Mame*, with Lucille Ball, Robert Preston and Bea Arthur, came to town. Younkers arranged special showings of each movie for customers, awarded door prizes and staged fashion shows. The one preceding *Mame* presented original costumes from the movie, modeled by Younkers associates. The showing of *The Great Gatsby* followed an evening-style show at the Capri Theater.[208]

A FUN PLACE FOR TEENS

Just as Younkers organized special events and celebrity visits to bring customers into the stores, it also staged elaborate activities to attract the all-important teen market. During the annual girls' state basketball tournament in 1978, the downtown Tea Room turned into a disco every Saturday afternoon between March 18 and April 22. Inspired by the 1977 hit movie *Saturday Night Fever*, "Saturday Afternoon Fever" for high school students included a KGGO disc jockey as master of ceremonies and dance instruction—sessions on couples dancing, touch dancing and the Latin hustle each ended with a dance contest. Along with food and prizes, Younkers gave away T-shirts, and KGGO distributed records. The event raised funds for both the teen board and their schools.[209]

FESTIVALS AND FUN

Programs that combined shopping with education and entertainment became increasingly ambitious in the 1970s. A two-week Younkers Carnevale d'Italia, from October 26 to November 7, 1970, brought customers into the downtown store to see a one-third-size replica of Michelangelo's Sistine Chapel ceiling. It had been created in Florence, Italy, and displayed at the Canadian World's Fair before coming to Des Moines. An elaborate faux-stone reproduction of the chapel was installed on the second floor to showcase the ceiling frescoes, and employees dressed as Swiss guards stood at the entrance to add atmosphere. (The installation traveled to Dubuque for Lent.) Customers could also experience the store's first-ever wine tasting party, sip espresso in a sidewalk café in the Tea Room foyer and watch Italian artisans demonstrate their crafts.[210]

Italy was followed by Great Britain, with a "fortnight" of activities from October 19 to November 2, 1974. The downtown and Merle Hay stores each hosted special events. Lord Snowdon, Anthony Armstrong-Jones (Princess Margaret's husband), was the special guest at a fundraising gala in the Tea Room, with dancing, cocktails and supper. The proceeds from the twenty-five-dollar tickets benefited the Friends of Educational Broadcasting. The next day, the royal celebrity opened an exhibit of his photography at the Merle Hay store.

The festival included the latest British fashions, daily style shows and temporary boutique shops offering British merchandise, antiques and art. Replicas of the Crown Jewels were displayed in the Tea Room foyer, and inside the restaurant, a daily show opened with Alfie Howard, the official town crier of the Greater London Borough of Lambeth, demonstrating his prowess as bell ringer and crier. He was followed by a parade of Younker associates dressed as Henry VIII and his wives, using costumes from the BBC TV production of *Henry VIII*. After a fashion show, Michael Sedgwick, a popular British singer, performed. Alfie Howard apparently enjoyed himself so much that he stayed to help open the new Store for Homes at Merle Hay Mall.[211]

The Merle Hay store hosted its own special events for the British festival: Sotheby Parke-Bernet sent a representative to give free appraisals of antiques and collectibles. British travel films, short features and full-length movies of Shakespeare's plays were screened in a theater set up on the second level at the mall. An actual British double-decker bus, with its own British driver, shuttled shoppers back and forth daily between the downtown and Merle Hay Mall stores.[212]

In 1979, a ten-day promotion in September focused on New York City and its fashion, food and ethnic diversity. Bill Blass brought his New York models and added local ones to present a style show in the Tea Room benefiting

The October/November 1984 issue of the *Younkers Reporter* regaled employees with the story of installing the seventeen-foot plaster replica of Michelangelo's *David*. MR.

David attracted thousands of customers to Younkers, many of whom had not been downtown for a long time.

17

The replica was the star attraction of Festivale Europa. *MR.*

the Des Moines Art Center. (A similar show at the Omaha store benefited the Joslyn Museum of Art.) Joe Namath signed autographs in the Younkers men's departments downtown and at Southridge Mall and presided over two benefit auctions.[213]

114

The 1984 extravaganza, Festivale Europa, was "the largest promotion ever in Younkers' 128 year history."[214] It involved the three Des Moines stores (downtown, Merle Hay and Southridge), two Omaha stores (Westroads and Center), two in Cedar Rapids (Lindale and Westdale) and the three stores in the Quad Cities (Bettendorf, Moline and Davenport). Organized under the leadership of president William Friedman Jr. and vice-president and general merchandise manager David Zelinsky, the event brought together European fashions, home furnishings, music and crafts. It was the culmination of more than a year of preparation, working with European buying offices and foreign commissions.

Festivale Europa launched at Westroads in Omaha with a Florentine banquet benefiting the Joslyn Art Center. The next day, Des Moines celebrated with a French banquet benefiting the Des Moines Art Center. Lord Patrick Lichfield, Queen Elizabeth's cousin and the official photographer for the British royal family, was a special guest at both. Lichfield appeared in Cedar Rapids at the Lindale store, too, and all three stores exhibited some of his best-known photos. In Cedar Rapids, a fashion show and lunch raised funds for St. Luke's and Mercy Hospitals. Alfie Howard, London's town crier, made a return visit. British and Italian artisans and French and Italian chefs all contributed to the lively sense of "something always happening" at Younkers.

The most remarkable attraction, however, was a seventeen-foot-tall plaster replica of Michelangelo's *David*. Packed in four separate cases, the statue was shipped from Italy to the downtown Des Moines store. It took eight to ten workmen nearly twelve hours, working all night, to uncrate and assemble the parts—and the assembly instructions were in Italian, so finding a translator slowed progress. Thousands of customers came to gawk at the replica. The 5,500-pound statue traveled to Gottschalk's retail store in Fresno after the Younkers event ended.[215]

These extravaganzas brought unique merchandise directly to Younkers from overseas sources and helped boost sales throughout the stores. Festivale Europa raised the bar on promotional spectacles so high that it was never surpassed. After 1985, changes in company leadership, strategic goals and the retail environment downplayed the importance of making the store a fun place to be and shifted the focus to the straightforward business of selling.

Chapter 12

A GREAT PLACE TO WORK

Throughout its history, Younkers has been described by its employees as a great place to work. In fact, many workers stayed there for their entire careers. In 1932, the 20-Year Club was established with forty-four employees who had been with the store since at least 1912 (and some since the 1890s). In 1972, the club numbered 269 members. By that time, membership in the club wasn't simply a nice honor. Members received additional vacation time, paid hospital and medical benefits and a greater share of the profit-sharing funds.[216] The longevity indicated a high degree of employee satisfaction and contributed to the store's stability and success.

BUILDING TEAM SPIRIT

Between 1874 and 1900, the sales staff was small enough that everyone knew everyone else, and it was not hard to generate a family feeling. As the store grew, especially through mergers and acquisitions in the 1920s, store-sponsored clubs, sports teams, activities and newsletters helped integrate new employees into the Younker family and build community spirit. Cribbage teams and bridge clubs, a Girls' Club, a Noodle Club, a Camera Club, a Young Men's Club and a Book Club helped create camaraderie and a social life that reinforced work ties. Younkers also fielded sports teams that competed with those of other companies in

Employees published a ring-bound "family cookbook" in 1990, with recipes from associates throughout the chain.

town. Commercial leagues for bowling, basketball, softball and golf encouraged team spirit outside work hours and benefited work relationships, too.

Like other department stores in the late nineteenth and early twentieth centuries, Younkers offered its single female employees vacation facilities at a summer camp. It was an affordable, supervised option that tapped into the new enthusiasm for healthful outdoor activities and gave young working women a respectable alternative to visiting family or staying at home for vacation. Unlike many stores back east, Younkers didn't own the campsite but arranged for Camp Dunlap, two miles from Madrid, to be available to its female employees at a cost of seven dollars per week or twelve dollars for two weeks.[217]

The company also hosted a huge holiday party every year, with a sit-down dinner either in the Tea Room and adjacent dining rooms or at the KRNT theater, with dancing and bingo following. In 1970, the company hired the famous Fred Waring and His Pennsylvanians to perform for the Des Moines employees, and dinner was replaced with cupcakes and popcorn; 2,500 people came.[218]

Ultimately, the point of fostering good morale and team spirit at any company is to improve work performance. Happy, loyal employees have a stake in the company's fortunes and take pride in making it successful. At Younkers, good morale came from something deeper. As Peter Taggart recalled, his father and William Friedman Sr. "were not only a great business team, they were best friends. Bill walked the floor with Dad the night I was born, and my middle name came from Bill." Employees' children met for play dates, and families vacationed together. "This was typical throughout the store," said Taggart. "Life-long friendships."[219]

Benefits

In the absence of paid sick leave and health benefits in the early years, employees formed the Mutual Aid Association to provide financial assistance to members who missed work due to illness. As membership grew, the MAA organized the credit union and underwrote the employee cafeteria, which offered hot meals at incredibly low prices. In 1953, the employees' cafeteria, which was on the seventh floor, served 163,705 meals at an average cost of about forty-five cents each.[220]

In 1940, the company introduced a hospital plan for employees, and in 1945, it instituted a profit-sharing plan to provide retirement income. The plan was pioneering and generous and cost employees nothing. All regular employees over twenty-five years of age who had been with the store for five consecutive years were eligible to participate. The plan was funded annually by a share of the store's pre-tax profits, which were deposited in a trust fund. The amount depended on annual store earnings and was determined by a firm of independent accountants following U.S. Treasury Department regulations. Employees who had come to Younkers from Harris-Emery or J. Mandelbaum & Sons could apply their years of continuous service at those stores to their Younkers service.[221]

The 1973 annual report credited the profit-sharing plan for contributing to the stability of the company's workforce, noting that Younkers had "one of the lowest management turnover rates in the country."[222] The commitment to promoting from within, adhered to since the company's founding, also encouraged employees to stay.

Equal Opportunity...to a Point

In 1880, Younkers hired the first female clerk in Des Moines, and by 1950, the store was employing more women and girls than any other business in town—and perhaps even the state. In 1932, the store introduced a new sales event, Women's Day, taking advantage of the leap year to stage a Sadie Hawkins–style role reversal. Women took over all of the executive and management positions and spearheaded the sales campaign. Although it was described as "a stunt, with jokes and good spirits combining to put it over," the women were, in fact, quite serious about staging a successful event.[223]

The sale received no advertising budget, but word of mouth proved effective enough to bring in the crowds, and the sale attracted attention from national retail magazines "both for its success and for the enthusiasm with which the women participated." The sale was repeated the next four years, but sales were hurt in 1933 by the emergency bank holiday, which froze all bank accounts for a week. In 1934, a blizzard discouraged business. The sale was held in 1940 (the next leap year) and 1942 but was dropped from the calendar in 1943, as were the other annual sales events.

In the 1940s, about half of the store's forty-some buyers were women. Women dominated the selling floor and moved into personnel, training and communications as well. At one time, the advertising department and print shop were entirely female. Finally, in 1985, the company hired its first female vice-president and general merchandise manager, Ginny Harris, and in 1992, Josephine Chaus joined the board of directors.[224]

In terms of race, Younkers, like most department stores, limited its employment of African Americans to jobs as porters, maids and warehouse workers before World War II. In the 1940s, the company sports teams were integrated, but holiday parties were not, and the sales floors and offices remained white until 1947, when the company made a commitment to hire African Americans for positions other than housekeeping and warehouse work. The first black sales associate was hired that year, and by the 1960s, African Americans represented 5 percent of the company's payroll—about half the percentage of African Americans in Des Moines. "The civil rights legislation created no panic for us," wrote Joseph Rosenfield, chairman of the board. "It only served to firm up our intention."[225]

Company president Charles Duchen maintained that "Younkers always has been way ahead of the game on the question of civil rights.… In 1952, when I first went to Sioux City as a manager, a call came in one day. It was from the store superintendent who was in charge of personnel, employee behavior, etc. He said, 'I hate to bother you with this since you're so new on the job.'" The manager of the store's restaurant, which was a leased business out of Kansas City, refused to seat a black family. Duchen told the superintendent to tell the manager to feed the family and to feed them well or turn in his resignation. Duchen was confident that "a similar situation never occurred again."[226]

Although the downtown Des Moines store failed to promote a black assistant buyer to the position of buyer until department stores elsewhere had paved the way, the company's Omaha branch received an award of merit from the Omaha Urban League in 1955. The citation noted that "the personnel department hires on the basis of qualifications alone," without regard to race or religion. By 1968, there were three African American assistant buyers, and longtime employee Frances Cuie had been promoted to art needlework buyer. When 20-Year Club member Mornetta Skipper retired in 1978, she had been a supervisor in all but three areas in the store. Black associates as well as white participated in the management trainee program, revised in 1985, which groomed participants for career growth at Younkers.[227]

In December 1970, in the wake of a tumultuous four years of racial unrest in Des Moines, Younkers agreed to participate in an experiment devised by students from the Des Moines Technical High School. A sophomore speech class had to design an "action project" and asked Younkers to install a black Santa during the times that the usual white Santa took his breaks. Sy Forrester, a homeschool advisor at Tech, agreed to play Santa, and the students observed people's reactions and interviewed customers. Student Charlene Holt reported that "about 75 per cent of the people were pleasantly surprised. About 20 percent couldn't have cared less. Only about five percent didn't like it." Forrester added, "I must have talked to about 1,000 kids, and not one said a thing about me being black."[228]

RETAILERS IN TRAINING

Over the 160 years that Younkers has been in business, it has given thousands of young people their first job, including a future governor (Robert Ray) and a future mayor (Preston Daniels).[229] In addition to the college, teen and advisory boards, which aimed to promote Younkers as a fashion authority for youth, the store developed relationships with high schools and colleges to help cultivate the next generation of merchants. The citywide High School Days brought in students to fill roles from president-for-a-day on down, including preparing ad copy for the newspaper and selling in the departments. The program was unusual enough that it won Younkers a nod for creative promotion from *Fashion Trades Weekly*.[230]

In the early 1940s, students could get a taste of the retail business through a six-week class and part-time jobs sponsored by the Des Moines Chamber of Commerce Retailers Bureau; they could take vocational training courses at the Des Moines Technical High School (now Central Campus); or they could enroll in Drake University, which introduced one of the few programs in the nation for a major in retailing.[231] Younkers supported all of these programs by accepting participating students as interns or part-time employees.

By 1976, the company was involved in at least ten educational programs, including Executive High School Internships of America, a two-year-old national project that paired students with employee mentors. The company also offered internships to students of various junior and community colleges and Iowa State and provided a GED program for employees who had not completed high school. Scholarship funds for Drake, Grinnell and Simpson students rounded out the company's support for higher education.[232]

Incentives such as the profit-sharing plan, training programs and opportunities for promotion made Younkers a good place to call home for hundreds of retail workers. The family feeling within the company spilled out into the community and helped weave the store into the fabric of its hometown.

Chapter 13

HERE TO DO WHAT IS RIGHT

Herman Younker's first newspaper advertisement in Des Moines in 1874 stated, "We have come to live here and mean to do what is right." While he had "honest goods at bottom prices" in mind, the words proved inspirational and prophetic. Over the ensuing decades, Younkers came to stand for good corporate citizenship, outstanding civic leadership and dedication to the well-being of the community, both in downtown Des Moines and in the towns and suburbs where it planted branch stores. A century after Herman Younker opened the Des Moines store, a poll of the city's residents showed that "Younkers headed the list of businesses and organizations most influential in community affairs."[233]

PUBLIC WELFARE

The policy of good corporate citizenship started early. In 1899, the *Daily Iowa Capital* noted, "No movement for the public good fails to secure aid from Younkers' [*sic*]. Every enterprise for the advancement of home interests is assisted by them, and they are liberal in their donations to the many charities which are constantly appealing to the people of cities."[234] In their personal lives, executives set an example, too. Sidney Mandelbaum helped found United Jewish Philanthropies (later the Jewish Welfare Federation of Des Moines) in 1914. Norman Wilchinski, a member of

Temple B'nai Jeshurun, gave liberally to many charities and as the store president "was always at the front in all endeavors for the public good." After his sudden death of a heart attack in the office in 1937, civic leaders and store employees alike mourned the loss of "one of Des Moines' most valuable citizens." His obituary noted, "He leaves as a priceless heritage the deep esteem and affection of his fellow citizens."[235]

Henry Frankel, who followed Wilchinski as president, also believed fervently in working for the common good and didn't mind haranguing employees to do the same. In November 1930 (when Frankel was still secretary-treasurer), he announced the upcoming weeklong Public Welfare Drive with this challenge: "Every Younker employee should, can and will want to aid this worthy cause that combines the raising of funds for all Public Charities in one great campaign. The funds that we contribute to these organizations guarantee an orderly community. They guarantee a community that is entitled to a proper degree of self-respect." Frankel didn't stop there, however. He went on to remind Younkerites that "a pack of chewing gum or a candy bar each week amounts to $2.50 a year. A small amount for you to deny yourself, but a needed help in this drive."[236]

The store's participation in the Public Welfare Drive "went over the top with a bang," noted the *Younker Reporter* the following month. "The subscriptions of Younker employees broke all previous records in the store, with a comparative increase between last year and this year of over 70%." The following year, the store achieved 100 percent participation, with employees pledging a total of $8,835.71. The company itself pledged enough to bring the total to 6 percent of the total Public Welfare budget.[237] And this was in the early years of the Depression.

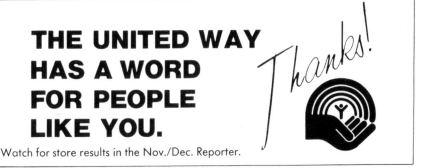

United Way's appreciation for the company's support. *MR.*

The Public Welfare Drive became Community Chest and eventually United Way, and Younkers continued to be a major contributor of money and personnel. In the 1950s, the corporation also made major donations to Methodist, Mercy and Lutheran Hospitals and pledged large sums to the Des Moines and Sioux City YMCAs.[238]

In the late 1970s, when walk-a-thons became a popular way to raise money for good causes, Younkers employees in Des Moines, Omaha and Sioux Falls participated in annual events to raise money for the Special Olympics programs in their respective states. In 1984, a few Younkers employees organized a Love Run to raise money for the Muscular Dystrophy Association. It later became the Jerry Lewis Muscular Dystrophy Association walk/run.[239]

Good deeds were good for their own sake, and they also helped the bottom line. Writing in 1955, then board chairman Joseph Rosenfield extolled employees for their generosity and public spirit, concluding, "All of these things are traditional with Younkers. It is an integral part of our philosophy, and the good will that it has engendered is one of our most priceless assets."[240]

SUPPORT FOR THE ARTS

Younkers enjoyed a special relationship with the Des Moines Art Center from its beginning in 1948. Henry Frankel, retired as president but still serving on the Younkers Board of Directors, was a trustee of the Edmundson Art Foundation Inc., which operated the Art Center. He also chaired the Art Center's fundraising committee in 1949, and it's likely he secured permission for the store to display five paintings from the permanent collection (including an El Greco) in the window at the corner of Seventh and Walnut to promote the membership drive.[241]

The store was also proud to have participated in furnishing the new building, which had been designed by famed International Style architect Eliel Saarinen. Florence Weaver and the decorating studio in the Store for Homes carried out the plans developed by Saarinen, which called for custom dyes for upholstery fabrics, special finishes for the furniture and handwoven draperies for the main foyer. Younkers workrooms made and installed the draperies, and the store furnished and applied the monks cloth that covered the gallery walls. "Altogether, the store feels a great pride in Miss Weaver's work in connection with a community project of such importance, and in the fact that Younkers

William Friedman Jr. (right) brought Halston to Omaha and Des Moines to benefit the Joslyn and the Des Moines Art Center. *Courtesy of Johnnie Friedman.*

decorating studios had a part in it," wrote the *Younker Reporter.*[242] Although Marcus Younker's son, Benjamin, wasn't involved with running the store, he, too, supported the Art Center with a gift of seventy-five prints by artists including Picasso, Chagall, Vlaminck, Maillol and Pissarro.[243]

In the 1970s, Younkers used its connections with top fashion designers and celebrities to raise funds for the Art Center and other local cultural institutions. These benefits, held in the Tea Room, typically featured an appearance by the designer, a fashion show and a cocktail buffet or dinner, followed by dancing and dessert at the Embassy Club for the top-level ticket holders. Bill Blass presented his fall collection for men and women in 1973 as the centerpiece of a benefit for the Cultural Trust Fund of the Greater Des Moines Community Foundation.[244]

Halston followed three years later, bringing his New York models to Des Moines to help the Art Center raise nearly $16,000. The Tea Room glowed

A chocolate moose, sculpted by Duffy Lyon of Butter Cow fame, tempted chocolate fans at a fundraiser for the Des Moines Ballet. *MR*.

with candlelight and throbbed with the beat of rock-and-roll music as the models put on a choreographed show, presenting swimwear, golf and tennis outfits, "slithery" jersey dresses and "virtuoso chiffons cut on the bias with lettuce-like rippled edges." Halston and his troupe had stopped in Omaha the night before on behalf of Younkers-owned Kilpatrick's and the Joslyn Museum. The funds in Des Moines supported the exhibition "Synchromism and American Color Abstraction 1910–1925."[245]

Younkers teamed up with the Des Moines Ballet Association and Friends of the Des Moines Ballet in October 1978 to present a fundraiser featuring Calvin Klein fashions. Younkers stepped up again to help the ballet in 1984 with a chocolate extravaganza in the Metropolis—forty thousand chocolate cakes, cookies, candies and jelly bellies piled high and available for sampling by some four thousand admission-paying visitors.[246]

In 1981, the award-winning fashion designer Geoffrey Beene brought his new spring resort collection to Des Moines, again benefiting the Des Moines Art Center. Two of his New York models strutted the Tea Room runway, showing off outfits inspired by English wallpaper and Beene's visit to Japan, as well as a daring dress made of ribbons alternating with transparent fabric.[247]

TEEN ACTIVISM

In the late 1960s and early 1970s, Younkers' teen and advisory boards took on service activities, reflecting the youth culture's demand for relevance and socially conscious activism. In 1971, the boards won second place in a national contest sponsored by *Seventeen* magazine promoting environmentalism. The teens spearheaded a drive to ban nonreturnable bottles and cans in Des Moines. The two youth boards used the award of $1,000 to make a donation to PACE Juvenile Center and buy a glass recycling machine for the city.[248]

THE FARM CRISIS

In the 1980s, a number of factors collided to produce the worst farm crisis since the Great Depression. Farmers who had taken on debt in the 1970s, when interest rates were low and prices for crops were high, found themselves impossibly squeezed in the 1980s when markets dried up and prices dropped. Farmers couldn't repay their debts, and thousands lost their farms. Musicians Willie Nelson, John Cougar Mellencamp and Neil Young

Younkers responded to the farm crisis of the mid-1980s by setting up an educational trust fund for future farmers. *MR.*

organized a fourteen-hour Farm Aid benefit concert at the University of Illinois–Champaign in 1985 and raised more than $9 million to provide relief, counseling services and legal aid to farmers in need.

Younkers responded to the idea immediately. Fred Hubbell, then CEO and chairman of the board, and Tom Gould, president, announced the establishment of the Younkers Farm Aid Agricultural Trust to provide scholarships for future farmers in the five states served by the store. The company opened the fund with 10 percent of one week's sales and secured additional contributions from vendors, Midwest businesses and farm organizations to raise $300,000. In 1986, twenty-four students from Iowa, Nebraska and Illinois received scholarships for the 1986–87 academic year.[249] The trust fund continues to award scholarships annually.

In 1955, chairman of the board Joseph Rosenfield wrote in the *Younker Reporter*, "Be a good citizen and participate in all worthwhile activities. This principle has been rigidly adhered to by Younkers during its entire history."[250] Younkers executives saw no contradiction between doing what was right and doing well as a business, and as Rosenfield noted, a healthy community made life better for everyone.

Chapter 14

THE END OF INDEPENDENCE

In August 1978, Younkers surprised the investment community—and everyone else—by announcing that it had made a deal with Equitable of Iowa Companies to be purchased. Corporate takeovers, especially hostile ones, repeatedly claimed the headlines in the 1970s and 1980s, and although the Equitable buyout of Younkers was friendly, it was still unusual for a retail business to be bought by an unrelated industry.

Younkers' retail empire was doing well and growing steadily, and the corporation's investments were doing even better, making Younker Brothers Inc. a tasty morsel for takeover. To stave off unwanted suitors, Charles Duchen, chairman of the board, resolved to find a local buyer who appreciated Younkers' place in the state and local community, was equally sound financially and would have no interest in the day-to-day running of a retail business. He approached Equitable's head, James Hubbell Jr., and a deal was struck. Equitable paid $72.2 million for all of Younkers' stock, and the deal was consummated in January 1979. Younker Brothers Inc. became Younkers Incorporated and had every expectation that business would proceed as usual.[251]

In 1981, then president William Friedman Jr. and his team took a careful look at Younkers' future customers. Data indicated that, nationally, baby boomers were coming into their own as drivers of the economy. They were better educated, had more discretionary income, knew what they wanted and emphasized getting good value for their dollar—which didn't necessarily mean the lowest price. "They will invest in the best quality level they can

The skywalk connected Younkers to the Kaleidoscope (owned by a subsidiary of Equitable of Iowa). *MR.*

afford providing the value image is there; hence the great importance of brand and store perceptions," the team found.[252]

A market study indicated that Younkers was not serving this group well, so management determined to focus on winning the loyalty of customers under age forty while continuing to serve the over-forty crowd. However, Younkers would no longer aim to be all things to all people. The five-year plan would move the company away from budget-priced goods and toward a greater emphasis on those at the moderate and "better" price points.[253]

Plans included major remodeling of five stores and fine-tuning of others to reflect the new direction for the company. At the downtown Des Moines store, the most dramatic change was the conversion of the basement, which had always housed the budget department, into the Metropolis in 1983. This trendy, upscale area consisted of specialty shops and boutiques, with services reminiscent of the store's heyday—the Younkers Flower Shop, a candy shop, the travel department, a bookstore, home furnishings, luggage and cameras all drew on the store's history as a provider of all kinds of services. Others—such as a potpourri shop, a gourmet grocery, artificial flowers and David's Cookies—were pure 1980s.[254]

At first, Equitable professed no interest in the running of Younkers, content to let the company do what it knew best, but then its executives decided that they were interested after all. Differences over strategy and management came to a head and ended with Friedman being dismissed in early 1985. The next president, W. Thomas Gould, came on board on July 29, 1985. Modernization efforts begun under Friedman continued, but Gould revised the target customer profile and merchandising categories. Now the fashion focus would be on three groups: Mainstream, Classic and Updated. Instead

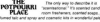

THE POTPOURRI PLACE The only way to describe it is "scentsational." It's scented candles, room fresheners, scented soaps, perfumed talc and spray and cosmetic kits in wonderful palettes.

Systems for Living . . . a complete collection of furnishings fit for today's lifestyles.

COBBLER SHOP It's the only place downtown where you can get your heels fixed while you wait. The **only** shoe repair place downtown is right here in The Metropolis.

Right: The Metropolis aimed to reach a young-adult, upscale customer. *MR.*

Below: Fine candies, a Younkers staple, were featured in the Metropolis. *MR.*

SERIOUS cook The Serious Cook . . . a superb setting for demonstrations of kitchen products, and quick lessons from the experts for preparing the perfect dinner . . . from pasta making to the 300 egg omelet (see DOWNTOWN People section). Modified from the pages of Metropolitan Home magazine, the Living Kitchen is a complete working kitchen featuring regular demonstrations of the latest cooking and baking equipment, unusual recipes and special culinary skills.

COBBLER SHOP

POST OFFICE

WRAP LABEL IT Buy the mailing materials and send your package right here. It's a one-stop operation. A great convenience for the busy downtowner.

of a broad selection of brands and vendors, there would be fewer labels but more depth in sizes and colors.[255]

In 1989, after four profitable years, Equitable decided to sell Younkers, but when no buyers appeared, Equitable took the company off the market. In 1992, Younkers and Equitable parted company amicably, and Younkers became a publicly held company trading on the stock exchange. Later that year, Younkers bought the privately owned H.C. Prange Company, a chain with twenty-five stores in Wisconsin, Michigan and Illinois.[256]

The addition just made Younkers Incorporated even more appealing to potential buyers. In October 1994, the company fended off a hostile takeover attempt by Carson Pirie Scott. In late 1995, the board of directors accepted a merger agreement with Proffitt's, a Tennessee-based company that operated Proffitt's department stores and McRae's as separate divisions. Younkers would keep its name and Des Moines headquarters.[257]

Proffitt's acquired Saks Holdings Inc. in 1998 and changed the company name to Saks Incorporated. As a Saks subsidiary, Younkers opened new stores in Michigan and began closing unprofitable ones in Iowa and Wisconsin. To the dismay of Des Moines city officials and residents, the new management gave up the company's historic connection to Iowa and moved the corporate headquarters to Wisconsin in 2002. The downtown Des Moines flagship store closed in August 2005, ending 106 years of continuous service in the same location.

To mark its closing, former and current employees and loyal customers crowded into the Tea Room on July 15, 2005, to share rarebit burgers and other Tea Room favorites. Letters, cards and memorabilia poured in from around Iowa and out of state with remembrances and salutes to the store. "I have wonderful memories of Younkers," wrote one former member of the art department. "The tea room, the rarebit burgers, the elevator operators, the basement, on and on. It was like a whole universe." "Fond memories at Younkers—they were good to their employees!" wrote another.[258]

On October 31, 2005, the York, Pennsylvania–based Bon-Ton Stores announced its agreement to purchase the Northern Department Store Group from Saks for $1.1 billion cash. The group included Younkers, Carson Pirie Scott, Herberger's, Bergner's and the Boston Store. (The sale wasn't completed until November 2006.)[259]

The downtown Younkers building remained empty until September 2013, when Wisconsin developer Alexander Company began renovations that would turn the building into 120 apartments with ground-level retail space. On March 29, 2014, however, a devastating fire destroyed the east building and left the west building badly damaged but salvageable. As of August 2015, investigators were unable to determine the cause but noted that embers left from renovation work couldn't be ruled out.[260]

Des Moines–based Blackbird Investments bought the property from Alexander Company in July 2015 and planned to renovate the surviving west half, renamed the Wilkins Building, into sixty apartments, with ground-level retail and underground parking. The company also planned to restore the Tea Room.

Younkers, unlike many of the great department stores that opened in the late nineteenth and early twentieth centuries, still survives as a brand, marking its 160th anniversary in 2016. Given the dramatic changes in where and how Americans shop, such longevity is a remarkable tribute— both to the pioneering and entrepreneurial Jewish families who founded and shaped it and to the community that loved and embraced it.

NOTES

DMPC City Directory = Des Moines and Polk County, Iowa, City Directory. *YR* = the *Younker Reporter*, briefly renamed the *New Younker Reporter* and, in 1980, *Younkers Reporter.* All issues of *YR* referenced in the notes are in the Younkers Inc. archives (YI), unless otherwise indicated. YI = Younkers Inc. (Younker Bros. Inc.) archives, MS2003.8, State Historical Society of Iowa, Des Moines.

Introduction

1. Lyn Oppenheim Foshé letter, July 15, 2005, Connie Boesen Collection; Elaine Estes interview by Vicki Ingham, June 19, 2015.

Chapter 1

2. Marcus Younker: Wolfe, *Notes from a Century*, 70–71.
3. Keokuk store: *YR*, April 1961.
4. Life in Keokuk: *The Buzzer*, 1926, YI.
5. Keokuk: Wolfe, *Notes from a Century*, 27, 33; Temple, *Younker Story.*
6. Knife story: *YR*, Autumn 1975, quoting Marcus Younker's account in the September 1925 edition of *The Buzzer.*
7. Peddling: *YR*, September 18, 1964; *YR*, December 1968.

8. Civil War: *YR*, April 1961.

9. Marriage: *YR*, June 1966. This issue of the *Younker Reporter* included a sixteen-page section, "The Younker Family History," compiled by William Temple, editor of *YR* for more than thirty-five years. He assembled a family history for the seventy-fifth anniversary in 1931, updated it for the centennial in 1956 and added a supplement in March 1969, when it was compiled as *The Younker Story*.

10. Des Moines trip: *YR*, September 1969.

11. Dissolution of partnership: *YR*, September 1969; Lipman's and Joseph's activities: Temple, "The Younker Family History," *YR*, June 1966; Lipman's Des Moines store: DMPC City Directory, 1879.

12. Ads from the *Daily Gate City*, September 30, 1874, and December 1874, reproduced in *YR*, September 1941.

13. Samuel's obituary: Temple, *Younker Story*.

14. Joseph Younker: Temple, "Younker Family History," see note 9.

Chapter 2

15. Des Moines: DMPC City Directory, 1866; historical population: Wikipedia, "Keokuk, Iowa," https://en.wikipedia.org/wiki/Keokuk,_Iowa.

16. Aaron Younker: *YR*, June 1966; DMPC City Directory, 1879.

17. Early ads reproduced in *YR*, August 1936.

18. L.M. Younker & Company: DMPC City Directory, 1879.

19. Wilchinskis: Temple, "Younker Family History," see note 9.

20. Mary McCann: *The Buzzer*, Seventieth Anniversary edition, 1926, YI.

21. Wikipedia, "Albert B. Cummins," https://en.wikipedia.org/wiki/Albert_B._Cummins; female employees, *YR*, March 4, 1933.

22. Memories: *The Buzzer*, Seventieth Anniversary edition, 1926, YI.

23. Wages: *YR*, March 4, 1933, and Rosenfield, "Personal View," 22.

24. Christmas gifts, Sam Hicks and cash boy memories in *The Buzzer*, Seventieth Anniversary edition, 1926, YI.

25. *Dry Goods Economist*, "Retail Merchandising Loses Pioneer."

26. Falk and Isaac: *YR*, Fall 1963; *The Buzzer*, Seventieth Anniversary edition, 1926, YI.

27. Falk: *The Buzzer*, see note 26.

28. Family at store: Temple, "Younker Family History," see note 9.

Chapter 3

29. Frankel's: Wolfe, *Notes from a Century*, 81–82.
30. Harris-Emery acquisition: Rosenfield, "Personal View," 22.
31. Harris-Emery ad: DMPC City Directory, 1892.
32. Harris-Emery: *YR*, September 1967.
33. *Daily Iowa Capital*, "Younkers Begin Work," April 8, 1899, 2.
34. *Des Moines Daily News*, "Destructive Fire: Harris-Emery Co.'s Large Retail Dry Goods Store Is Food for Flames," October 3, 1899, 1.
35. Ibid., "Younkers' Open: Great Store of the Great Mercantile Firm Opens Tomorrow," November 8, 1899, 1; *Daily Iowa Capital*, "Younkers' Opening," November 9, 1899, 4.
36. *Daily Iowa Capital*, "Younkers' Opening."
37. *Des Moines Leader*, "New Store Opens Today," November 9, 1899, 3.
38. 1909 expansion: Jacobsen, National Register form, section 8:17.
39. Jacobsen, National Register form, section 8:19.
40. Ibid., section 8:20–21; *YR*, September 1967.
41. The Grand: *YR*, September 1973.
42. *Des Moines Evening Tribune*, "Younkers Will Occupy Block-Long Store," October 16, 1922, 1; Wilchinski's presidency: *Annals of Iowa*, "Norman Morris Wilchinski," 156–57; *YR*, August 1937.
43. Jacobsen, National Register form, section 8:22.
44. Harris-Emery and Younker relations: *YR*, December 1967.
45. Merger deal: Rosenfield, "Personal View," 51.
46. Rosenfield on board: *YR*, August 1951.
47. Records of Incorporation, Merger, Acquisitions etc. and Stock Records, YI.
48. J. Mandelbaum & Sons: *YR*, September 1967; Wolfe, *Notes from a Century*, 64; DMPC City Directories, 1866–99.

Chapter 4

49. Slogan: *YR*, November 1931.
50. Great Engineering Achievements of the 20th Century, "Air Conditioning and Refrigeration Timeline," http://www.greatachievements. org/?id=3854; Great Engineering Achievements of the 20th Century, "Air Conditioning and Refrigeration History-Part 2," http://www. greatachievements.org/?id=3859; Whitaker, *Service and Style*, 102.
51. Leopold: *YR*, February 26, 1936.

52. Air conditioning benefits: *YR*, February 26, 1936; June 1936.
53. *New York Times*: Whitaker, *Service and Style*, 103.
54. Multi-level stores: Whitaker, *Service and Style*, 93.
55. Wikipedia, "Escalator," en.wikipedia.org/wiki/Escalator.
56. Westinghouse brand: *YR*, November 1939.
57. Radio script for escalator unveiling, Miscellaneous Subject Files, YI.
58. Song: *YR*, November 1939.
59. Frankel: *YR*, November 1939.
60. Charga-Plates: *YR*, June 1956.

Chapter 5

61. Frankel: *YR*, December 1941.
62. E bonds and war stamps: Kimble, *Mobilizing the Home Front*, 23–24; F and G bonds: Treasury Direct, "Other Treasury Securities," www.treasurydirect. gov/indiv/research/indepth/other/res_othersecurities.htm.
63. United States American History, "United States History: U.S. War Bonds," u-s-history.com/pages/h1682.html.
64. Payroll deduction: *YR*, February 26, 1942.
65. "America needs us": *YR*, June 3, 1942.
66. Bond shelter: *Good Morning* special edition, July 17, 1942, YI; *YR*, April 1946.
67. Quota exceeded: *YR*, August 28, 1942.
68. Frankel: *YR*, June 3, 1942.
69. Windows, events and displays: *YR*, September 17, 1943; *YR*, October 1943; *YR*, February 18, 1944.
70. Bond sales: *YR*, April 1946.
71. War stamp dresses: *YR*, February 18, 1944; *YR*, February 16, 1945.
72. Service members: *YR*, June 3, 1942; *YR*, May 19, 1945.
73. Wikipedia, "Women's Army Corps," https://en.wikipedia.org/wiki/ Women's_Army_Corps.
74. Outfitting WAACs: *YR*, August 28, 1942.
75. *YR*, August 28, 1942.
76. Services: "Younkers and Des Moines," booklet prepared for Women's Auxiliary Army Corps members at Fort Des Moines, Promotional Materials, YI.
77. Wikipedia, "Women's Army Corps," see note 73.
78. WAColony: *YR*, October 26, 1944; *YR*, November 17, 1944.
79. Shortages: *YR*, February 16, 1945.

80. Strategies: *YR*, April 9, 1943.
81. South American shop: *YR*, August 20, 1943.
82. Bible ad: *YR*, February 16, 1945.
83. End of war: *YR*, August 17, 1945.
84. Stocking distribution system: *YR*, March 1946, YI.

Chapter 6

85. While companies such as Macy's and the May Company grew through acquisition of other stores in the immediate postwar period, growth through suburban branches bearing the same name as the downtown flagship store came more slowly, picking up speed in the 1950s and 1960s. Whitaker, *Service and Style*, 25–26.
86. Rationale: *YR*, March 1945.
87. Sostrin: *YR*, October 1947.
88. Younker-Davidson's: *YR*, September 18, 1964; *YR*, Summer 1964.
89. Innes, Daniel Fisher: *YR*, January 1956; *YR*, November 1957.
90. Sostrin: *YR*, August 21, 1959.
91. The Center: *YR*, January 1954; *YR*, September 18, 1964.
92. Kilpatrick's: *YR*, September 18, 1964; *YR*, March 15, 1968.
93. Merle Hay: *YR*, July 1956; *YR*, August 1959.
94. Eastgate: *YR*, Spring 1962.
95. Hours: *YR*, Christmas 1962; *YR*, March 1970.
96. Sales volume: *YR*, Summer 1964.
97. Fires: *YR*, December 1969.
98. Ron Cohen, "Ten Die in Explosion, Fire at Younkers Store," *Women's Wear Daily*, November 7, 1978, News Clippings and Articles, 1977–83, YI.
99. Jim Healey, "Chemical Reaction Tied to '78 Younkers Fire, Outside Experts Agree," *Des Moines Register*, March 10, 1979, News Clippings and Articles, 1977–83, YI.
100. Evan Roth, "Younkers Fire Ruling Is Overturned," *Des Moines Evening Tribune*, September 22, 1982, News Clippings and Articles, 1977–83, YI.
101. Charles Corcoran, "Firms Sued in Younkers Fire," *Des Moines Evening Tribune*, November 5, 1980, News Clippings and Articles, 1977–83, YI.
102. Richard Paxson, "Younkers Reopens Store at Mall without Ceremony," *Des Moines Sunday Register*, October 21, 1979, News Clippings and Articles, 1977–83, YI; William Friedman Jr., interview.
103. Auto business: *YR*, March 28, 1960.

104. *Fashion Trades Weekly*: *YR*, October 1946.
105. Sales volume: *YR*, January 1950; *YR*, Summer 1974.

Chapter 7

106. Bryson, *Life and Times*, 25.
107. Whitaker, *Service and Style*, 225–26.
108. *YR*, January 1944. Incident shared with *YR* columnist by Pearl, a Tea Room waitress, who was the cashier in the restaurant where she overheard this conversation.
109. Tea Rooms description: *The Buzzer*, January 1926, YI.
110. Wikipedia, "Roger Williams (pianist)," https://en.wikipedia.org/wiki/Roger_Williams_(pianist).
111. Doc Lawson: *YR*, November 1931.
112. Tea Room as community institution: *YR*, July 1949.
113. Whitaker, *Service and Style*, 229.
114. Included in *Adventures in Good Eating*: *YR*, November 1954.
115. Tea Room specialties: *YR*, November 1954; *YR*, "Bountiful Buffet," October 1960.
116. Foyer modernization: *YR*, February 1953.
117. Cremona Room: "Younkers Grows with Iowa," Younkers' Ninetieth Anniversary/Iowa's centennial commemorative booklet, 1946, YI; *YR*, September 1964.
118. Garden Buffet: *YR*, November 13, 1940.
119. Rose Room: *YR*, June 1959.
120. Rose Room décor and murals: *YR*, January 1960.
121. Kitchen staffing: *YR*, July 1949.
122. Branch store restaurants: *YR*, Spring 1963, *YR*, January 1981.
123. Cinnamon roll secret ingredient: Peter Taggart interview. Bake shop: *YR*, July 1949; prize-winning bakers: *YR*, Autumn 1975.
124. Sweet Shoppe: *YR*, December 1973.

Chapter 8

125. House furnishings in 1899 store: Younker Bros. ad, *Des Moines Leader*, November 9, 1899; 1924 furniture sales ads: *Des Moines Register*, August 7 and August 30, 1924.

126. Sostrin: *YR*, June 3, 1942.

127. Friedman interview.

128. Taggart interview.

129. "Times Change!" ad; Friedman quote in "Younkers Open 'A New Kind of Store for a New Kind of Home'" newspaper clipping; "No swimming seas" quote in Rose Roberts, "The Ads Are Saying," *Retailing Home Furnishings*, July 8, 1946; all from Younkers Store for Homes Scrapbook, MS2010.12, YI.

130. Store contents: *Furniture Index*, "Younkers Sets a Record," July 1946, Miscellaneous Subject Files, YI.

131. *Des Moines Register*, "30,000 Visit New Store for Homes," June 12, 1946, Younkers Store for Homes Scrapbook, see note 129; Taggart interview.

132. Mrs. Ralph Moorehead, "15,000 in First Five Hours Jam Opening of Younkers Unit," *Retailing Home Furnishings*, June 17, 1946, Younkers Store for Homes Scrapbook, see note 129.

133. Brands: *YR*, February 1953.

134. Modular furniture: *YR*, February 1948.

135. Peter Taggart e-mail to Vicki Ingham, January 25, 2016.

136. Decorating: *Ye Christmas Buzzer*, 1927, YI; Windsor Terrace apartments: *YR*, November 13, 1940.

137. Home counselor: *Good Morning: Employees' News of the Week*, April 8, 1940, YI.

138. *Chicago Market News*, Younkers Store for Homes Scrapbook, see note 129.

139. Service department business: *YR*, April 1955.

140. Home planning: *YR*, February 1946.

141. Smiley, "Making the Modified Modern."

142. Fleur Cowles, "A Home to Live in Now," *Look*, April 27, 1948, in Younkers Store for Homes Scrapbook, see note 129.

143. Newspaper advertisement in Younkers Store for Homes Scrapbook, see note 129.

144. Wikipedia, "Lustron House," https://en.wikipedia.org/wiki/Lustron_house.

145. Store for Homes scrapbook; ad from *Des Moines Sunday Register*, June 6, 1948, in Younkers Store for Homes Scrapbook, see note 129.

146. Store for Homes scrapbook, "Dream House Opened by High Officials," newspaper clipping, Younkers Store for Homes Scrapbook, see note 129.

147. Merle Hay rationale: Taggart interview; store description: *YR*, Autumn 1974.

148. Furniture Warehouse: *YR*, September 21, 1973.

Chapter 9

149. Alterations policy: *YR*, April 1982.
150. Services available: "Will You Giftwrap My Hippopotamus?" 1971 customer service booklet created by participants in the Thirty-third Retail Operations Course, *YR*, June 1971.
151. Flower shop: *YR*, July 1948.
152. Younkers candy: *YR*, July 1948; Betty Jones Duncan, "Younkers," Connie Boesen Collection.
153. Sewing facilities: *YR*, June 1941.
154. "Younkers and Des Moines," booklet prepared for Women's Auxiliary Army Corps members at Fort Des Moines, Promotional Materials, YI.
155. Travel services: *Good Morning*, January 18, 1937, YI; *YR*, July 1980; *YR*, December 1981.
156. Mail-order service: *YR*, March/April/May 1984, Margaret Rubicam Collection; "Younkers Grows with Iowa," Younkers' Ninetieth Anniversary booklet; WAAC booklet, YI.
157. Corsetry by mail order: *YR*, "Komments by Kutch," January 1950; Susan Chira, "Post-Hirohito, Japan Debates His War Role," *New York Times*, January 21, 1989.
158. Delivery figures: *YR*, April 1954.
159. Free delivery: *YR*, April 1960; *Des Moines Register*, "Younkers Reluctantly Drops 'Won't Be Undersold' Policy," December 10, 1981, News Clippings and Articles, 1977–83; "Will You Giftwrap My Hippopotamus?" YI.
160. For You: *YR*, December 1988.
161. Capacity Day: *YR*, June 1931.
162. Sostrin on "Satisfaction Always": *YR*, March 1961.
163. Customer satisfaction: *YR*, March 1961; Leonard Sloane, "Iowa's Younkers: Friendly Store," *New York Times*, April 11, 1966, YI.
164. Mrs. Hazel Patterson: *YR*, October 1950.
165. Ames shopper: *YR*, February 15, 1946.
166. Happy customer: *YR*, Fall 1991.
167. Sioux Falls customer: *YR*, Winter 1991.

Chapter 10

168. Intern's comment: *YR*, Spring 1976.
169. First fashion tea: *The Buzzer*, March 1926, YI.

170. Fashion shows: Whitaker, *Service and Style*, 141.

171. Bill Peverill's modeling debut: "Stories from 'Pipa Bill': Younkers Tea Room," Connie Boesen Collection.

172. Younkers models: *The Buzzer*, October 6, 1927, YI; *Good Morning*, November 1, 1937, YI; *YR*, June 1947.

173. Younker-Davidson's fashion shows: *YR*, March 1959; *YR*, April 1960.

174. *The Best of the West*: *YR*, April 1978.

175. *The You You're Looking For*: *YR*, May 1979.

176. Amos Parrish: Taylor, *Inventing Times Square*, 102–3.

177. Other consultants: Taylor, *Inventing Times Square*, 103; Parrish clinic closure: *Guide to the Amos Parrish Fashion Merchandising Clinic* workbook, 1930, Kellen Design Archives, the New School Archives and Special Collections, http://library.newschool.edu/archives/findingaids/KA0111.html.

178. Farrell's buying trip: *YR*, March 4, 1933; Veneman's trip: *YR*, February 27, 1935.

179. Trouser suits: "1930s Fashion—The Year of Wearing Trousers—1932," June 15, 2014, www.glamourdaze.com; Berry, *Screen Style*, 143–46.

180. Trouser suits at Younkers: *YR*, March 4, 1933.

181. Frances Perkins: *YR*, December 1934.

182. California Collection: *YR*, May 1946.

183. National advertising: *YR*, October 1946.

184. Corsetry French Room: *YR*, February 1934.

185. Sostrin: *YR*, February 16, 1945; *Fashion Trades Weekly*: *YR*, October 1946, YI; fashion umbrella: Friedman interview.

186. French Room: *YR*, October 1948; Raymond Loewy, "The Father of Industrial Design: Raymond Loewy," http://www.raymondloewy.com/about.html.

187. Nettie Rosenstein: Harriman, "Profiles," 28.

188. French Room customer: *YR*, January 1950.

189. Omen at Adrian's: *YR*, July 1952; Wikipedia, "Adrian (costume designer)," https://en.wikipedia.org/wiki/Adrian_%28costume_designer%29.

190. 1953 French Room items: *YR*, September 1953.

191. Millinery French Room: *YR*, September 1953.

192. Branch French Rooms: *YR*, March 1971.

193. Fur department: *YR*, October 1948.

194. Sadie Byrd: *YR*, June 1953.

195. Ads for college women's clothes: *Des Moines Sunday Register*, August 17, 1924; new hi-teen department: *YR*, February 27, 1934; Strawbridge & Clothier: Whitaker, *Service and Style*, 282.

196. Teen and advisory boards: *YR*, Summer 1975, *YR*, June 1969.
197. Buyers to Europe: *YR*, Spring 1962; *YR*, March 1969.

Chapter 11

198. Peverill, "Stories from Pipa Bill," Connie Boesen Collection.
199. Issues of the *Younker Reporter* noted that window displays were created especially for the store; purchases from Marshall Field: Friedman interview.
200. Jean Keiter quote: *YR*, December 1978.
201. Swander: *YR*, November 1947; May 1954.
202. Kodel tennis tournament: *YR*, August 1979; "Something Always Happening": *YR*, June 1957.
203. College Club entertainment: *YR*, December 1931.
204. Theater Nights: *YR*, February 1937.
205. Czech dinner: *Good Morning*, March 25, 1940, YI; South American evening: *Good Morning*, January 6, 1941, YI.
206. Elevators: *YR*, August 1985.
207. Movie tie-ins: *YR*, February 27, 1940; *YR*, September 21, 1945.
208. *Mame* and *Gatsby* tie-ins: *YR*, Summer 1974.
209. Saturday Afternoon Fever: *YR*, April 1978.
210. Carnevale d'Italia: *YR*, December 1970.
211. British "fortnight": *YR*, Winter 1974.
212. British festival at Merle Hay: *YR*, Autumn 1974.
213. Best of New York: *YR*, October 1979.
214. Festivale Europa: *YR*, August–September 1984.
215. Michelangelo's *David*: *YR*, August–September 1984.

Chapter 12

216. 20-Year Club: *YR*, February 26, 1932; benefits: *YR*, December 1969.
217. Summer camp: *The Buzzer*, June 1925, YI.
218. Holiday party: *YR*, December 1970.
219. Taggart e-mail to Vicki Ingham, January 25, 2016.
220. Mutual Aid Association: *The Buzzer*, 1940, YI; *YR*, November 1954.
221. Profit-sharing plan: *YR*, April 20, 1945. Herman and Aaron Younker had introduced an early profit-sharing plan in 1908, when the articles of incorporation were amended to create a class of stock called Second

Preferred Stock. Shares were non-voting and available only to employees "for the purpose of encouraging them in saving of their earnings and encouraging a spirit of loyalty to the corporation and its interests." This class received guaranteed dividends of up to 6 percent annually, with the incentive of an additional 5 percent per year for employees with more than five years of service. If an employee left the company for any reason before the end of a five-year period, the company would have the right to buy the shares back at par plus 6 percent from the date of the last dividend paid. The second-preferred stock category was reaffirmed in the 1911 amendment but not thereafter, so the plan must have been discontinued by 1912. See Records of Incorporation, Merger, Acquisition, etc., YI.

222. Stability: *YR*, Summer 1974.

223. Women's Day: *YR*, February 27, 1935.

224. Employing women: statistics from Les Suhler, subscription department manager of *Cowles Magazines*, *YR*, January 1950; first female vice-president: *YR*, December/November 1985; board of directors: *YR*, July 1992.

225. Rosenfield, "Personal View," 53.

226. Restaurant story: *Comment*, "Charles Duchen Understands 'People Business'," April 1973, Des Moines: Bankers Life Company magazine, reproduced in *YR*, September 1973, Connie Boesen Collection.

227. Omaha Urban League: *YR*, March 1956; Mornetta Skipper: *YR*, March 1978; management training: *YR*, September/October 1985.

228. Black Santa experiment: *YR*, March 1971.

229. Future governor, mayor: David Elbert, "One Last Celebration," *Des Moines Register*, July 9, 2005, 1D, 6D.

230. High School Day: *YR*, June 4, 1941; *Fashion Trades Weekly* article, reproduced in *YR*, October 1946.

231. Chamber of Commerce classes: *YR*, February 16, 1945.

232. Student intern program: *YR*, Spring 1976.

Chapter 13

233. Poll: *YR*, Summer 1974.

234. *Daily Iowa Capital*, The Capital, "Younker Contribution," February 3, 1899, 4.

235. Mandelbaum: *YR*, March 1959; Wilchinski: *Annals of Iowa*, "Norman Morris Wilchinski," 156–57; *YR*, August 1937.

236. Frankel on Public Welfare drive: *YR*, November 1930.

237. Drive results: *YR*, December 1930; results, 1931: *YR*, December 1931.

238. Hospital donations: *YR*, April 14, 1955.

239. Love Run: *YR*, August 1980; *YR*, June 1986.

240. Rosenfield: *YR*, April 15, 1955.

241. Art Center membership drive: *YR*, April 1949.

242. Art Center décor: *YR*, April 1948.

243. Benjamin Younker gift: Temple, "Younker Family History," *YR*, June 1966.

244. Bill Blass: *YR*, December 1973.

245. Halston benefit: Sara Giovanitti, "Season Gala: Halston Show," *Des Moines Register*, November 2, 1976; exhibition: *YR*, August 1978.

246. Ballet fundraisers: *YR*, October 1978; *YR*, December 1984.

247. Beene: Jim Blume, "Avoid Fashion Fads, Beene Urges," *Des Moines Register*, December 6, 1981, 3B.

248. Teen activism: *YR*, June 1971.

249. Farm Aid: *YR*, June 1986.

250. Rosenfield: *YR*, April 15, 1955.

Chapter 14

251. Sale rationale: Friedman interview; sale details: Encyclopedia.com, "Younkers Inc.," http://www.encyclopedia.com/topic/Younkers_Inc.aspx.

252. Customer analysis: *YR*, January 1982.

253. Five-year plan: *YR*, February 1982.

254. Metropolis: *YR*, February 1982.

255. Leadership and strategy change: *YR*, January/February 1986.

256. Prange purchase: *YR*, December 1992.

257. Takeover attempt and merger: *YR*, December 1994; *YR*, Winter 1995.

258. Farewell party: unsigned postcard and "Younker Memories," by Carolyn Cole Beery, Omaha, Connie Boesen Collection.

259. Bon-Ton purchase: Investor Relations, "The Bon-Ton to Acquire 142 Stores from Saks Incorporated for $1.1 Billion in Cash," October 31, 2005, http://investors.bonton.com/releasedetail.cfm?ReleaseID=260759; *Des Moines Sunday Register*, "Timeline of the Historic Building," Metro edition, March 22, 2015, 14A.

260. Fire: *Des Moines Sunday Register*, March 22, 2015: 14A; KWWL, "Investigators Cannot Determine Cause of Younkers Fire," August 4, 2015, http://www.kwwl.com/story/29704279/2015/08/04/investigators-cannot-determine-cause-of-younkers-fire.

BIBLIOGRAPHY

Annals of Iowa 21, "Norman Morris Wilchinski" (1937): 156–57. http://ir.uiowa.edu/annals-of-iowa/vol21/iss2/10.

Berry, Sarah. *Screen Style: Fashion and Femininity in 1930s Hollywood*. Minneapolis: University of Minnesota Press, 1997. https://books.google.com/books?id=mTwmMRwXll8C&pg=PA142&lpg=PA142&dq=screen+style+fashion+and+femininity+in+1930s+hollywood&source=bl&ots=LXB8BCBZPd&sig=bB_U441HEntfekmrXLn88_eyrbc&hl=en&sa=X&ved=0ahUKEwjvpPfwwKLKAhWJeD4KHWOJAwYQ6AEIUzAJ#v=onepage&q=screen%20style%20fashion%20and%20femininity%20in%201930s%20hollywood&f=false

Bryson, Bill. *The Life and Times of the Thunderbolt Kid*. New York: Broadway, 2006.

Des Moines and Polk County, Iowa City Directories, 1866–1922.

Dry Goods Economist. "Retail Merchandising Loses Pioneer in Death of Herman Younker" (September 4, 1920): 20. https://books.google.com/books?id=G8RFAQAAMAAJ&pg=PA20&lpg=PA20&dq=Herman+Younker+obituary&source=bl&ots=Jj2mJCHUUa&sig=j_tuhDd96rTRBMrVr8ZAnDX7aGo&hl=en&sa=X&ved=0ahUKEwiArs6PkpbKAhVHNiYKHYMVCaMQ6AEIHDAA#v=onepage&q=Herman%20Younker%20obituary&f=false.

Estes, Elaine. Interviewed by Vicki Ingham, June 19, 2015.

Friedman, William, Jr., former Younkers president and CEO. Interviewed by Vicki Ingham, July 24, 2015.

Harriman, Margaret Case. "Profiles: Very Terrific, Very Divine." *The New Yorker*, October 19, 1940. http://archives.newyorker.com/?i=1940-10-19#folio=028.

Harris, Leon. *Merchant Princes: An Intimate History of Jewish Families Who Built Great Department Stores*. New York: Kodansha America, 1994.

Jacobsen, James E. National Register of Historic Places registration form, nomination for Younker Brothers Department Store, filed January 13, 2010. Iowa State Historic Preservation Office, Des Moines.

Kimble, James J. *Mobilizing the Home Front: War Bonds and Domestic Propaganda*. College Station: Texas A&M University Press, 2006.

Lindaman, Matthew. "First the War, Then the Future: Younkers Department Store and the Projection of a Civic Image during World War II." *Annals of Iowa* 73 (2014): 1–27. http://ir.uiowa.edu/annals-of-iowa/vol73/iss1/2.

Rosenfield, Joseph. "A Personal View of Younkers History." *Iowan* 16, no. 4 (n.d.): 20–23, 51–53.

Smiley, David. "Making the Modified Modern." In *Housing and Dwelling: Perspectives on Modern Domestic Architecture*. Edited by Barbara Miller Lane. London: Routledge, 2007. https://books.google.com/books?id=dmp_AgAAQBAJ&pg=PA290&lpg=PA290&dq=Adirondack+homes+1948&source=bl&ots=p8HBvzl6bd&sig=F_e7ma4t2Hl9JgJH9yT776NgDLA&hl=en&sa=X&ved=0CFAQ6AEwDGoVChMIt6q8-8ONyAIViXQ-Ch1kqQvQ#v=onepage&q=Adirondack%20homes%201948&f=false.

Taggart, Peter. Interviewed by Vicki Ingham, September 30, 2015.

Taylor, William R. *Inventing Times Square: Commerce and Culture at the Crossroads of the World, 1880–1939*. New York: Russell Sage Foundation, 1991. https://books.google.com/books?id=KPqCt8W4CB8C&pg=PA102&d

q=Amos+Parrish&hl=en&sa=X&ved=0ahUKEwjG2tbrvaLKAhVEyj4
KHfyIBw0Q6AEIUTAJ#v=onepage&q=Amos%20Parrish&f=false.

Temple, William. "The Younker Story," 1969. Compiled Younkers History Information, Younkers Inc.

Whitaker, Jan. *Service and Style: How the American Department Store Fashioned the Middle Class.* New York: St. Martin's Press. 2006.

Wolfe, Jack. *A Century with Iowa Jewry: As Complete a History as Could Be Obtained of Iowa Jewry from 1833 through 1940.* Des Moines: Iowa Printing and Supply Company, 1941.

Younkers Inc. (Younker Bros. Inc.). MS2003.8 collection and MS2010.12. State Historical Society of Iowa, Des Moines.

INDEX

A

air conditioning 29–31
Amos Parrish Fashion Clinics 93
architecture, flagship store 22, 25
art shows 109
auto business 52

B

bakery 63
Book Corner 80
branch stores 46, 47, 49, 51

C

candy at Younkers 78
celebrity events 107, 111, 125
Charga-Plate 33
college boards 102
Cremona Room 61, 64
custom clothing 100
customer satisfaction policy 84, 85

D

delivery services 18, 82, 83
designer clothing 98
Des Moines Art Center 62, 114,
     115, 124, 126
Duchen, Charles 119, 129

E

Eastgate self-service store 50
employee benefits 116, 118
Equitable of Iowa 129
escalators 31

F

fashion shows 58, 87, 91, 102,
     103
festivals and events 111, 112, 115
fires 51, 132
flower shop 78
Fort Dodge 46, 47, 73

Frankel, Henry 26, 28, 30, 34, 36, 46, 123, 124
Frankel's 20
Franklin, Omar 47
French Room 87, 96, 97, 98, 99, 100
Friedman, William, Jr. 52, 115, 129
Friedman, William, Sr. 66, 117
furniture sales 25, 65, 66, 67, 74
Furniture Showroom Warehouse 74

G

Garden Buffet 61, 63, 64

H

Halston 87, 95, 125
Harris-Emery 20, 21, 25, 26, 56, 81, 118
home decorating services 66, 71, 73
home planning services 66, 72

J

Jean Sardou photo studio 80
J. Mandelbaum & Sons 26, 28, 118

K

Keokuk 11, 13, 14, 15, 16
Kilpatrick's 49, 63, 126

L

Lustron homes 73

M

mail order 42, 44, 81, 83
Mandelbaum, Sidney 28, 122
Mason City 46, 47, 91
mergers and acquisitions 25, 26, 48, 132
Merle Hay Plaza/Mall 49, 51, 63, 74, 83, 112, 115
Metropolis 126, 130
millinery 95, 99
Mr. Blandings Builds His Dream House 73

N

"New Escalator Song" 32
1948 Look House 73

P

Personal Service Bureau 77
philanthropic activities 123, 124, 125, 126, 128
profit-sharing plan 118

R

racial equality 119, 120
"Read Your Bible" 42
restaurants 59, 61, 63, 64
Rosenfield, Joseph 26, 46, 119, 124, 128
Rose Room 61, 64

S

shoe repair 77
shopping centers 48, 49

Sostrin, Morey 46, 49, 84, 85, 96, 97
Stark Travel Service 80
Store for Homes 52, 66, 67, 68, 71, 72, 74, 75, 112
Swander, Maurice 106

T

Taggart, Robert 67, 71
teen boards 102, 127
teens 101, 111, 120
Theater Nights 108
20-Year Club 116, 120

W

WAACs 39, 40
war bond campaigns 34, 35, 36, 37
war stamp dresses 38
wartime rationing 41, 44
Wilchinski, Norman 17, 19, 24, 26, 27, 28, 122
Wilkins Building 23, 25, 56, 133
Wilkins Department Store 23, 25
Williams, Roger, and Tea Room 58
window displays 37, 105, 111
women, hiring of 17, 118
Women's Day 118

Y

Younker, Aaron 16, 18, 26, 27, 54
Younker-Davidson 48, 92
Younker, Herman 11, 15, 16, 17, 18, 26, 27
Younker, Lipman 11, 14, 15, 17
Younker, Marcus 11, 13, 14, 15, 18, 125

Younker, Samuel 11, 14, 15, 16
Younkers Tea Room 51, 54, 56, 58, 60, 61, 63, 64, 87, 93, 97, 108, 109, 111, 112, 125, 126, 132, 133
youth market 101, 102

ABOUT THE AUTHOR

Now a freelance writer, Vicki Ingham spent nearly thirty years in book and magazine publishing as a staff editor/writer. While her work focused on home decorating, Christmas, crafts and gardening, her interest in the history of art, architecture and decorative arts led her to pursue a master's degree in art history mid-career. She is a member of Preservation Iowa, the National Trust for Historic Preservation and the Des Moines Art Center.

Also by Vicki Ingham

Art Meets Fashion (Des Moines Art Center)

Illuminated History: Stained Glass at the Cathedral Church of St. Paul
(Des Moines)

Art of the New South: Women Artists of Birmingham, Alabama, 1890–1950
(Birmingham Historical Society)

Currently writing articles for Cottage Journal *and* dsm *magazine, including feature stories on artists, craftsmen, gardens and gardeners, homes and more.*

Books for Meredith Corporation, including Flea Market Decorating, New Classic Style *and* Color Solutions.

Books for Oxmoor House, including Elegance in Flowers, Christmas with Southern Living *(annual) and* Home for the Holidays.